Hire
the
American
Dream

LESSONS FROM DOMINO'S PIZZA—WHERE
DELIVERYMEN BECOME MILLIONAIRES

Hire
the
American
Dream

HOW TO BUILD YOUR MINIMUM WAGE
WORKFORCE INTO A HIGH-PERFORMANCE,
CUSTOMER-FOCUSED TEAM

DAVE MELTON AND TIM MCINTYRE

WILEY

JOHN WILEY & SONS, INC.

Published by John Wiley & Sons, Inc., Hoboken, New Jersey
Published simultaneously in Canada

For general information on our other products and services or for technical support, please contact our Customer Care Department within the United States at (800) 762-2974, outside the United States at (317) 572-3993 or fax (317) 572-4002.

Wiley also publishes its books in a variety of electronic formats. Some content that appears in print may not be available in electronic books. For more information about Wiley products, visit our web site at www.wiley.com.

Library of Congress Cataloging-in-Publication Data:

Melton, Dave, 1959-

Hire the American dream : how to build your minimum wage workforce into a high-performace, customer-focused team / Dave Melton and Tim McIntyre.

p. cm.

Includes bibliographical references and index.

ISBN 978-0-470-43828-2 (cloth)

1. Employee motivation—United States. 2. Working poor—United States. 3. Minimum wage—United States. I. McIntyre, Tim. II. Title.

HF5549.5.M63 2009

658.3—dc22

2009004167

Printed in the United States of America

10 9 8 7 6 5 4 3 2 1

To my parents and to Angie: Your love and support have made it all possible. To all DPNY team members, past and present: Thanks for making my dreams come true.

—Dave

Love to my sons, David Paul and Ethan John. This is for Lynn Baldwin—te amo.

—Tim

Contents

Foreword

I joined Domino's Pizza in 1999 as chairman of the board and chief executive officer. The company had a rich history and hundreds of successful franchisees, many of whom had made millions owning and operating pizza delivery stores. What I found especially remarkable was that so many of those franchise owners had started their careers as pizza delivery drivers, often making a minimum hourly wage, plus tips, and had worked their way up to become owners. Entrepreneurial spirit and the American Dream were alive and thriving throughout our stores. I was excited to join this team.

However, there were still challenges to confront and opportunities to pursue. For example, employee turnover astounded me. After meeting with the senior leader in human resources on my first day, I learned that we were averaging 158 percent turnover across our system! At that time, this meant we had to recruit, hire, and train approximately 180,000 people every year! How could that be? We had created a "revolving door" culture as a result of our sloppy assessment and hiring practices throughout the organization.

I had just come from a company where turnover was in the low single digits, and we had been named to *Fortune* magazine's "100 Best Companies to Work For" three consecutive times. I was very proud of that, and couldn't fathom the idea that at Domino's we had to put up with such high turnover throughout the organization. How could I build a strong culture and drive growth and quality improvements when the team was constantly changing? Constantly hiring and training new team members is expensive, time-consuming, and not in anyone's best interests. We had to do something.

I asked the vice president in charge of human resources to analyze turnover and work with me to come up with ways to reduce it—drastically. At first, his skeptical response puzzled me. Our turnover numbers, he said, weren't that bad compared to many other companies in our industry. What's the big deal? Then, the more I thought about it, it made me angry. Essentially, he told me that this was "the way it is" and that I should get used to it.

No wonder we had 158 percent turnover! I got rid of him.

I rallied the team, and together we took on the challenge of battling the turnover epidemic. It wasn't money that was making people leave. It was the culture in the stores . . . the way people were being treated, the training and support they *weren't* getting, and the lack of encouragement to become entrepreneurs in their own stores. It was also clear that there was no consistent system in place to make sure that we were hiring the *right* people. Because the company had grown so much in the previous several years, store managers and franchisees were hiring virtually anyone who came into the stores with a valid driver's license and car insurance, without taking the time to assess whether they were a good fit for the company. I called it, "warm-body hiring!"

After researching the issue and looking at the strengths and weaknesses of our competitors as well, I announced at a company convention of Domino's owners and managers that, "the pizza company with the best people will win," and I meant it. We began to create systems to screen applicants better, to interview and assess talent in ways that were relevant to job performance, and to ensure we developed a culture in our stores that was welcoming, supportive, and focused on developing our team members. We began showing them how they could achieve their career goals at our company, whether it was pizza delivery, management, supervision, or owning their own franchise. We also began purging our system of the negative-energy managers who were contributing to turnover by driving away good employees.

We formalized a Vision Statement and a set of Guiding Principles that formed the foundation of everything else we did and shared them with everyone we could.

Our Vision: *Exceptional franchisees and team members on a mission to be the best pizza delivery company in the world.*

Our Guiding Principles:

One brand. One system. One team.
➤ Putting people first.
➤ Demanding integrity.
➤ Striving to make every customer a local customer.
➤ Delivering with smart hustle and positive energy.
➤ Winning by improving results every day.

In the 10 years since we've embarked on this mission of reducing turnover and improving the quality of our team members, we've made significant progress. Voluntary turnover at the hourly employee level is half of what it was when I started. Managers are sticking around longer and more of them are actively pursuing franchise opportunities. We have lowered turnover at virtually every level of our company. We don't compare ourselves to the "average" players in our industry; we benchmark against the very best in class in the area of employee turnover. I am sure we will never get turnover rates as low as I want them to be . . . but we will never stop trying!

I learned early on that Dave Melton had "cracked the code" in his New York City franchise. His employees, who are mostly immigrants to the United States, are extremely loyal and committed to customer service. The average tenure of hourly employees in his stores is more than eight years. His four store managers have been with him at least a decade, and in the past six years he's not had to replace a single store manager. Each of them started as an hourly worker delivering pizzas on a bicycle for minimum wage plus tips— and now each manages a million-dollar business. They are part of a culture centered on teamwork and rewards, as Dave has an incentive program that motivates his team to succeed.

My experience has taught me that to be a great leader you have to be a coach and a teacher. Great leaders lead by example and articulate a vision. They find out how people want to be treated and treat them that way. Leaders motivate their teams, celebrate their successes, and challenge them to reach greater heights. Leaders are not afraid to ask questions and learn what they can from others. They are not afraid to admit that they don't have all the answers just because they're in charge.

Dave is a wonderful example of this, and as a result, he has succeeded in an extremely tough market. When he started, nobody believed that Domino's could succeed in New York City, the most competitive and celebrated pizza market in the world. Dave eventually came to oversee six stores, even though it took him some time to make it happen. He learned many lessons along the way, which he is sharing in this book. Today he is one of the most recognized and respected franchisees in the Domino's system. His reputation for customer service and exceptional team members is acknowledged throughout the world. Dave has done us the service of providing so many of his ideas in the pages of this book. Enjoy—and don't be afraid to steal any of them for your own business!

—David A. Brandon
  Chairman and Chief Executive Officer
  Domino's Pizza, Inc.

Acknowledgments

This book represents a career full of great experiences. Several significant lights went on in my life: meeting my wife, meeting Frank Meeks, and considering New York City as a place to start my first franchise. I'm grateful that I recognized the importance of these events. I'd like to thank the team members in our stores; they work hard every day to delight our customers. There are thousands of great Domino's Pizza people around the country from whom I learned how to run great stores and who shared their experiences with me. I thank them for the knowledge and the inspiration. My appreciation to Patti Wilmot, Scott Hinshaw, Asi Sheikh, Zakir Safi, Emir Lopez, Zia Shah, and Shaik Shamin for the interviews and the insight. To Don Meij, Tony Osani, and Glenn Mueller for their contributions. I'd also like to thank Richard Narramore, senior editor at Wiley, for believing that my story was worth telling. Thanks to Tim McIntyre, although it took me three times to convince him that he was the right guy to help me write this book.

—Dave Melton

I have the greatest job: telling stories about some of the coolest people on the planet. Thanks to 120,000 Dominoids worldwide who do what they do every day. Thanks to Dave Brandon and Lynn Liddle for their support of this project, their leadership and friendship; and to the Communications team at Domino's for their creativity and amazing energy. Thanks, of course, to Dave Melton for the chance to work on this book, although I turned him down twice.

—Tim McIntyre

Introduction

What Kind of a Manager Has Zero Turnover in the Fast-Food Industry and Turns Minimum-Wage Employees into Millionaires?

Recruiting, hiring, and retaining minimum-wage employees is a monumental task for businesses, large or small. It's not uncommon for managers to fill the same position in their workforce two, three, four, or more times a year because minimum-wage workers don't work out or they move on to something "better." Minimum-wage workers sometimes don't show up for work because they don't feel like it, or they can be rude to customers, or they may find other ways of making a supervisor's life difficult. Does it really have to be this way?

What if I told you there was a pizza shop owner in New York City who has close to zero turnover, has an average employee tenure of eight years, and has seen some of his minimum-wage employees go on to become millionaires? What if this guy put all of his secrets into a book to help others like him overcome the challenges of employing minimum-wage workers? Hard to believe? Let me introduce you to Dave Melton.

I met Dave in 1994, less than five years after he opened the first franchised Domino's Pizza stores in Manhattan. While many people predicted failure for Domino's in the town known for "New York pizza," Dave, in his eagerness and optimism, saw something different: a city of millions, filled with nothing but opportunity.

The first time I saw him, Dave was hustling and sweating as he led members of his team to deliver pizzas to the NBC studios in Rockefeller Center. Domino's was the title sponsor of NBC's NFL halftime show at the time, which meant that every Sunday, Domino's was feeding the crew and the on-air talent, including Ahmad Rashad and Mike Ditka. Dave was leading the charge, running through the lobby into the elevator, then dashing down the halls to the studio. He was energetic, enthusiastic, friendly, and convinced he was going to be a millionaire franchisee some day.

Today, he is. His four stores in Manhattan generate more than $4 million in sales every year. He is constantly looking to grow, and, as I write this, Dave has just purchased two more stores in Connecticut. Those stores will not just help him build his business, they will provide opportunities to some of his highly qualified and hungry assistant managers who want to take the reins of their own stores. So far, five of his managers, who started delivering pizza for minimum wage, have gone on to become franchisees themselves. Four of them have become millionaires, and they own nearly 20 stores between them—the American Dream come true. Dave's current store managers, who don't yet have franchises of their own, are also big success stories: After arriving in America from countries all over the world and starting at minimum wage, they are all now making $60,000 to $80,000 a year and have entered the middle class, thanks to hard work, ambition, and taking advantage of the opportunity Dave and Domino's have provided. One of his grateful employees even named his son "Melton" in honor of Dave. This is an amazing honor, but it's less surprising once you see Dave in action with his employees and the way he makes them feel respected, trusted, and important. These are some of the lessons you'll learn in this book: not only how to do these things, but why.

Dave's biggest "problem" is one that makes him unique among people who manage entry-level, minimum-wage workers: He has virtually zero turnover. The managers of his four stores have been doing their jobs for at least six years. There is a long waiting list of people who are eager to start working in one of his stores as soon as a position becomes available. The best way for his dedicated crop of qualified assistants to grow, then, is for Dave to open more stores. They don't want to leave to work for other franchisees—they're loyal to Dave. That's unheard of in the fast-food industry. If you manage frontline or minimum-wage workers, you might be able to learn a few things from him!

In this book, you'll read not just the story of how Dave confronted the challenges of selling pizza in New York City and how he turned his immigrant-based, entry-level, hourly employees into a loyal team, you'll find a lot of ideas that you can implement in your business today, from customer service tips to ideas for incentivizing your team to succeed beyond your expectations.

Dave's wife, business partner, and co-CEO is Angie, and they recently celebrated their twenty-fifth wedding anniversary. Dave is the operations guy, the customer service fanatic, and the creative force; he bounces from one topic to another. Angie is his complement—down-to-earth, focused, pragmatic, but equally energetic; she handles the company's finances and personnel administration.

Dave opened his first store in Manhattan in 1989, a market Domino's had previously not been able to enter with any success.

Before taking this big step, he visited the city. "I just kept looking at all of those buildings, all of those people," Dave says. "I realized my sales could be as high as these skyscrapers. I thought if I could run my stores the way I did at my first store in Virginia, there was no way I could fail."

The reality, of course, was a lot tougher than he ever imagined. New Yorkers aren't like "everybody else." The cultural adjustment for a polite young man from small-town Virginia was difficult, and he was especially unaccustomed to the raw edge in native New Yorkers. But his biggest challenges that first year were hiring and employee turnover. He had no experience dealing with New York's biggest pool of hourly employees—its burgeoning immigrant population—and most of his minimum-wage employees didn't buy in to Dave's customer-service orientation, standards, and work rules. Gradually, he cracked the code, and the secrets are laid out in this book. For example, one of the first ways he found to build a great team was to get rid of people!

By 1995, Dave had opened his fourth store and had begun to see the fruits of his labor. His team was beginning to gel and he was becoming more confident as a business owner. He ran for president of the Domino's New York marketing cooperative (whereby all stores in the market contribute money to a pool, make marketwide promotion decisions, and buy local advertising more cost-effectively). "At the time, the co-op was a joke. There were 90 people contributing money, and they all wanted a say in the decisions and the votes. Meetings took forever and very little was accomplished,"

Dave told me. "I ran [for president] by guaranteeing that the meetings would start and end on time or everyone in the room would get $3, just like Domino's was guaranteeing 30-minute delivery or $3 off. People thought it was funny, but I got elected."

The meetings became more effective almost immediately. Dave pushed to have the large, unwieldy co-op create a 10-member board of directors, elected by their peers. The board would be the ones to speak at meetings and vote on the decisions. "We went from being a joke to becoming the largest co-op with the most stores, the highest average sales, and one of Domino's most successful markets. It was a surprising turnaround, and a great accomplishment."

But Dave's proudest achievement is his role in helping to create the American Dream for so many of his employees. "I love seeing my people become successful," Dave says. "That's what happened to me, and it's created so much personal satisfaction to see these guys come through my system and go on to become wildly successful themselves." Knowing that he has been able to do the "impossible" and that he could help others to do the same is what led Dave to write this book and share the lessons he's learned over 25 years with people who face the same challenges so that they can achieve their dreams. Dave has been a high-profile personality in the community of Domino's Pizza for years. If you name an award in the franchise system, Dave has won it at least once. He's served on national advisory boards, covering topics from marketing to supply chain services. He's a member of the company's franchise leadership council and has served as chairman of an association of Domino's franchisees. He and Angie have developed such a solid team in Manhattan, they are able to travel extensively, to meet and share best practices with other Domino's franchisees around the world.

When he's not working, you'll find Dave on adventure trips, fishing, golfing, biking, kayaking . . . or beekeeping, at his home in Connecticut. "One of the things I've discovered is that beekeeping is a lot like management. You have to make good decisions. If you manage the hive well and give it the right kind of resources, the bees reward you with honey. A few years ago, I got 60 pounds of honey from my four hives. I brought a couple of jars to a meeting and donated it to a charity auction—the jars ended up generating $1,000 for a very good cause."

While much of what Dave does is public at Domino's, perhaps the real measure of his character as a manager can be found by talking privately to his team members. One of his team members, an immigrant from Pakistan, told me about a time when he was struggling to save money to buy a laptop computer for his younger brother so that his brother could be more successful at school. The employee got up the courage to ask Dave and Angie for a loan. They turned him down. Instead, they went out and bought a fully loaded laptop and gave it to the employee to present to his brother. The gesture still brings tears to the employee's eyes when he tells the story. I worked for months with Dave on this book, but this is a story he never told me. I presume the gesture was something that came so naturally to him, he didn't think to mention it. I think the lesson here, and in much of this book, is that if store managers and owners can implement some basic principles to find the right people and motivate them to succeed, give them opportunities to be promoted, and show some personal interest and concern, the results can be tremendous—not only far lower turnover, and better performance, but also the incredible satisfaction of helping others achieve the American Dream.

—Tim McIntyre

Hire
the
American
Dream

Chapter 1

Domino's Pizza, New York City—Coaching Frontline Workers to Succeed in the World's Toughest Pizza Market

If you manage minimum-wage or entry-level workers, you know that it's very difficult to motivate a person who might be planning to work for you for only a month or two. You've probably also made some of the same mistakes I did in my first year running a Domino's Pizza store in New York City: If you are desperate for workers, you might not check references like you should; you might take "prior experience" notes on the application at face value; you might not pay enough attention to applicants' demeanor in your interviews, if you even take much time to interview at all. As for me, during my first year I was too busy trying to field a team with *any* players, so I took on some people who weren't right for my business. Sound familiar?

When I opened the first franchised Domino's Pizza store in New York City in 1989, I was young and hungry, eager to succeed, and ready to take on the toughest pizza market in the world. I was also intimidated. While I had great training and eight years of management and store operations experience in Virginia and Washington, D.C., before I opened my first store, I was not quite prepared for how challenging New York would be or how hard I would have to work to succeed.

Based on my experience of opening many Domino's Pizza stores in new markets, I knew it would be tough finding dedicated workers willing to start at minimum wage—workers who were not out to rip me off; workers who cared how they treated customers and who didn't behave as if coming to work on time was merely a suggestion. I knew that in the fast-food industry the annual turnover rate for minimum-wage front-line employees was an astounding 150 percent, but I thought I could do better. My previous experience as a Domino's store manager had provided me with solid training for recruiting, hiring, and supervising entry-level employees. In my stores in Virginia I had always been able to find people who were able to see the business the way that I saw it: as a great opportunity with a fun company in a growing industry. But the reality on 89th Street and Third Avenue on the Upper East Side nearly put me out of business in my first year.

It started off well enough. I recruited some friends and colleagues to come work in New York while I opened that first store, and for the first few months things went extremely well. Based on the store's opening weeks—we were averaging more than $20,000 a week in sales—it was on pace to produce sales of $1 million a year right off the bat. *If you can make it here, you can make it anywhere!* I thought. I was having a ball. I was confident enough in those early months to open a second store, this time on First Avenue and East 74th Street. This time, nothing worked. The customers in the new market were a bit older, and they were wealthier—we didn't have as many of the young, single pizza customers as we did on 89th Street. I didn't know how different neighborhoods could be in Manhattan. We worked hard, but it took seven months to get that store up to $10,000 a week—about half of my goal of $1 million in annual sales. I worked in the First Avenue store nearly 80 hours a week for 200 days straight without a break. It was brutal, painful work. My one solace was my store on 89th Street . . . or so I thought.

With my attention completely focused on my second store, things began to fall apart at the first one. I thought I had a good core of people working for me, but it turned out that the core was rotten. I relied on store managers who ultimately didn't have the same goals as I did to recruit and hire new people, and I paid for it in team members who didn't treat my business the right way. In my absence, some of my employees were blatantly stealing from me, while the others were unmotivated, unreliable, unfriendly to customers, or all three.

Despite my early mistakes, I knew good frontline employees were the key to running a successful business. I needed employees who behaved as if they owned the company, who really cared about every aspect of the business, just like I did. But how do you find those people when you're offering only minimum wage?

I started by practicing and focusing on some fundamental management principles that most people agree with, at least in theory:

➤ Understanding that hiring is the most important investment in your business
➤ The importance of treating people right
➤ Believing that you work for your customers
➤ Making sure that every product you sell is the best it can be
➤ Sharing your success with the employees who help make you successful.

Most managers would agree with these ideas in theory, but it's amazing how few are able to put them into practice.

Once I started trying to implement these basic principles in my business, it took some time for my new team members to believe what I was saying, to trust in my vision of the business. I had to prove that I really would share the financial success of the stores with them. It also took a little time to convince them that the standards I had really weren't merely suggestions . . . that this was the way we were going to do business, and if they didn't accept that, they couldn't work for me. It was difficult, but doing these things consistently allowed me to build a solid core of employees in each of my stores—employees who take pride in their jobs. Today, we have a deep team with dozens of dedicated employees who enjoy the fruits of their labor, thousands of loyal customers who call back time after time for a great Domino's pizza, and a business I couldn't be more proud of.

Over the years, I figured out some employee management secrets I want to share with you in this book. These helped me and my wife, Angie, grow our business into four successful Domino's Pizza franchises in one of the toughest pizza markets in the world. All of our stores are in Manhattan, the heart of New York City, where we face stiff competition from authentic, family-owned Italian restaurants and pizza shops on virtually every corner. Our stores generate over $4 million in sales annually. That is a lot of pizza—and a lot of happy customers who come back again and again. But the most rewarding thing is that our employees have been able to share in our success.

■ HIRING THE AMERICAN DREAM: MOVING MINIMUM-WAGE WORKERS INTO THE MIDDLE CLASS—AND BEYOND

Because my stores are in New York City, most of my employees are immigrants, and for some of my team members, this is their very first job. Sometimes their ability to speak English is not great when they first arrive. Some are still in high school and don't have a work history. For some hiring managers, this would be enough reason to look elsewhere for employees. Yet working with this labor pool, I've created a great team of managers, each of whom has been on my team for at least *10 years*. This is in an industry with a 51 percent annual turnover rate at the management level. In the past six years, I've had *zero* turnover on my management team. All of my managers started as hourly workers delivering pizzas on a bicycle—earning minimum wage plus tips. Now their compensation is $60,000 to $80,000, which includes a percentage of their location's profits. As an entrepreneur and an American, nothing has made me prouder than being able to help my employees work their way up from minimum wage and into the middle class and beyond. Want to talk about job satisfaction? Several of my team members who started as deliverymen, people like Jim Denburg, Emir Lopez, Anthony Maestri, and Rob Cookston, have gone on to become millionaires. That really makes me feel great.

What's my secret to creating a great team of employees? Each chapter in this book describes a part of it, but the following list provides a summary:

1. I share my vision for my stores with all my employees. I sell them on why I think Domino's is a great place to work.
2. I treat my employees with respect.
3. I provide them with support and accommodate their special needs when I can.
4. I offer them performance incentives and opportunities for promotion.
5. I teach them to think like business owners.

The purpose of this book is to help any current or aspiring business owner or manager find high-quality, low-wage employees and teach them the basics of customer service and incentive pay so that they become successful, long-term contributors. Employees want money, opportunity, friends, respect, and fun. If you can teach your frontline employees the basic principles of great business, including customer service, loyalty, motivation, and the entrepreneurial spirit, you will inspire them to achieve incredible results for themselves and for you. Every enlightened business owner can benefit from the energy, commitment, and loyalty that entry-level employees and immigrant workers have to offer. Many of these people want to work hard and make a better life for themselves, if someone will just give them the opportunity. This information is not theoretical, textbook stuff. It's not a bunch of golden nuggets I'll be sharing from "on high." This is real. Angie and I live this stuff every day.

■ HOW I STARTED IN THIS BUSINESS

I started working for Domino's shortly after I graduated from James Madison University in Virginia. Many of my best friends were starting careers as accountants or attorneys . . . and I became the "pizza guy." There was no end to the ribbing I took when we got together, especially because my friends could not believe that I would use a college degree for a job that required me to wear a uniform and a name tag. Where was my pride? Today, I take pleasure in good-naturedly reminding them that they continue to work office jobs, while I'm in the position of *hiring* accountants and attorneys to work for *me*.

My first job at Domino's was as a minimum-wage manager-in-training, which featured many hours of delivering pizzas. Like most of my peers, I hadn't planned to be at Domino's Pizza for very long. It was 1982 and I had just graduated from James Madison. I'd spent a few months working at a bank and realized that the environment there wasn't for me. After the bank "freed up my future," I spent a few more months looking for that perfect opportunity—the one that would start the rest of my career. I looked at a bunch of jobs, but nothing inspired me much. Then one morning my girlfriend Angie woke me up with six words I'll never forget: "Get a job . . . or get out." Now that was inspiring!

Angie's dad published a newspaper in Prince William County, Virginia. As I looked in the want ads, one caught my eye. A pizza company I'd never heard of, Domino's, was looking for managers-in-training. There were only 500 Domino's stores in the United States at the time, which explained why I hadn't heard of them before. What I liked was the promise that general managers would make 25 percent of the profit of the unit they managed. I sent in a resume to Frank Meeks, who was the corporate area supervisor of the store, and he called and asked me to come in for an interview on Sunday. *What kind of company does interviews on a Sunday?* I wondered. Well, Frank worked for Congressman Trent Lott in D.C., but on the weekends he enthusiastically supervised one of the few Domino's shops in the Virginia/Maryland area.

Now I was really impressed, and intrigued, because here was a very successful guy just a couple years older than me who was working in D.C.; he had been student body president at Ole Miss and president of his college fraternity; he could have been a lawyer, a politician, virtually anything he wanted—and yet he was totally pumped up about Domino's Pizza!

I liked that I would be in a management training position almost immediately, and after I took the job I found out that I would be given as much responsibility as I could handle. The feedback about how I was doing my job was immediate: Sales were either going up or they weren't. If I was doing my job well, then food and labor costs would be in line, and I'd be able to know it that very night. I also liked that I was in a position where I worked with my hands, creating great-tasting (and great-looking) pizzas, and working with a lot of people, who—like me—wanted to make money. The hard work and camaraderie clicked for me, too. It was exhausting, exhilarating work—and I loved it!

One of the first things Frank taught me was the importance of each customer. The customer was my real boss, not him. He said to me, "The number one way to grow sales and profits is exceptional customer service. We should do everything we can to make every customer happy, because that customer could become a customer for life and spend as much as $1,000 a year with us." For a pizza guy, that was thinking big.

Soon I was promoted to store manager, with the responsibility of hiring and training my own team. Now, not only my supervisor, but I wanted sales and profits to increase, because I was going to get a piece of the action (or a piece of the pie, so to speak). My team and I worked hard; we set sales records, and together we became the most profitable store in the region. I began to see what my future could be like! I knew then and there that I wanted to own my own Domino's franchise—and that I was going to become a millionaire. I moved up the ladder, becoming a supervisor of several stores, then a vice president of operations, with several supervisors reporting to me. I built a few dozen stores in Virginia and D.C. as the director of development for Frank and another Virginia franchisee, Dave Wood. I learned a lot about hiring, training, and leadership, and I was getting some great experience for the next chapter in my career.

I started looking for an area in which to become a franchisee. I went to North Carolina, Massachusetts, New Jersey, and a few other markets, and then Brad Biggers, a friend of mine who was also a Domino's franchisee, suggested Manhattan. I'd never been to New York City before, so the only thing I knew about Manhattan was from the movies and the news. I came to the city and walked around eating pizza slices from dozens of the ubiquitous pizza shops, and I believed that we could compete with our product, and especially with our service. That's when I set my mind on conquering the Big Apple.

What I learned as a store manager—the importance of providing exceptional customer service, making a great product, maintaining a crisp image, being proud of being the "pizza guy"—inspired me and helped form the foundation of how I run my own franchise today.

■ BRING ENTREPRENEURIAL SPIRIT AND OPPORTUNITY TO YOUR MINIMUM-WAGE WORKERS

One of my themes in this book is the importance of hiring "nice people," the strength of attitude over experience, passion over skill. I'll also talk about the importance of creating a "common language" of incentives and rewards that all of your employees can understand, no matter how many jobs they've had, where they're from, or what their first language is. You'll find out about how to make sure your employees have the same kinds of entrepreneurial opportunity that got me excited about the business.

In my case, it's not hard to make sure my frontline employees have the chance to earn a share of profits, because that kind of thinking is encouraged within the Domino's organization. The company's founder, Tom Monaghan, was a great entrepreneur and found ways to build entrepreneurial spirit and rewards into the culture and the business.

For example, most of his franchisees didn't just buy their way in. They started out like me, with no money, delivering pizzas. He wouldn't allow people to become franchisees until they had managed a pizza store for at least a year, and they all started out delivering pizzas to customers.

Tom was also an innovator; he traveled all over, often sleeping in his car, to learn the "secrets" of every pizza shop owner from Michigan to Manhattan. He built a company that revolved around hiring good people and treating them well, around handling the rush and making great pizzas fast, and around the power of incentives to drive individual performance. He preached ethics and honesty and service. He wanted only people with "pizza sauce running through their veins." When Tom chose to retire and sell the company in 1998, it was worth over $1.1 billion. Not bad for a guy who started a pizza shop just trying to earn a buck or two for school.

During the first five decades of the company's expansion, hundreds—thousands, maybe—of minimum-wage pizza delivery men and women have gone on to own their own stores and become millionaires—including some of my own employees. Today, Domino's Pizza has more than 8,700 pizza stores, most of them owned by independent entrepreneurs like me, in over 60 different markets across the globe.

Throughout this book, I'll share the lessons I've learned in greater detail by introducing you to some great Domino's Pizza people who are living examples of what it means to have "pizza sauce running through your veins." Some have been working in my New York City Domino's Pizza stores since 1996, and they have become valuable assets to my franchise. They came to the United States with a vision for a brighter future for themselves and for their families. They found themselves at Domino's Pizza, in a minimum-wage job, but with opportunity ahead of them. I was able to help them see the opportunities because I had lived them myself. In the process I found myself some wonderful employees who have helped me delight my customers. All this time, I was just trying to run my business the best way I knew how. I didn't realize it at the time, but I was *Hiring the American Dream*.

Chapter 2

Don't Hire Warm Bodies—Hire Warm People!

Shaik Shamin was born in Bangladesh. He came to the United States in the mid-1990s; he was young, inexperienced, and a bit nervous when he walked into my 32nd and Third Avenue pizza shop looking for a job in 1996. Like me years before, Shamin wasn't necessarily looking to make Domino's Pizza his life's career choice. He was a young man in a new country, and he was looking for an entry-level job so he could earn some money to help his family. We hired him because during the interview process he smiled and said thank you, and I could tell he really meant it. Those are little things, but they are extremely important in the customer service business—which is the business I'm really in. You're in this business too, if you hire or manage any customer-facing workers, whether you manage a restaurant, a movie theater, a car wash, or a grocery store. Smiling and saying thank you are two things I look for as part of my hiring profile. This was inspired by something Domino's founder Tom Monaghan once said: "You can succeed if you can do all the little things well. And the biggest little thing you can do is simply be nice to people." I hire employees who know how to be nice to my customers.

■ ATTITUDE IS MORE IMPORTANT THAN EXPERIENCE

How do you find the nice ones? "There is no *one* way to learn about a prospective employee," says Patti Wilmot, executive vice president of PeopleFirst at Domino's. She has more than 35 years of human resources experience. "You might be interviewing the shiest, most timid person ever and they surprise you by becoming one of your best employees. On the other hand, you may be sucked in by someone who's outgoing and gregarious, only to find that they're not interested in working very hard."

However, you can tell a great deal about prospective employees during that first interview if you pay less attention to what they're saying than to how they're behaving. The frontline employees you're hiring are the face of your business. Wouldn't we all rather to do business with a smiling face than with an unsmiling one?

Most people are going to be nervous during a job interview, of course; that's not what you should be looking at. Instead, pay attention to these details:

➤ Do they look you in the eye?
➤ Do they smile?
➤ Do they seem excited about the potential to work for you?
➤ Are they friendly?
➤ Do they say thank you?
➤ Does their personality come through?
➤ Do they seem eager to learn?
➤ Do they express interest in growth opportunities?
➤ Do they possess the entrepreneurial spirit?
➤ Do they like serving other people and making them happy?

Attitude is more important than skill, because you can teach a skill but you can't teach a friendly, positive attitude. Patrick Doyle, president of Domino's USA, put it this way, "The person who has the biggest impact on how an employee treats a customer is not you . . . heck, it's not even themselves. *It's their mom."* (And, yes, dad, too.) The foundation of a person's character was built long before he or she comes to you for employment. You cannot build anything of significance on a shaky foundation—especially if you want it to last. This is why I will hire attitude over experience every time.

Most people are giving you their absolute best in a job interview (or should be), and if they're not friendly with you under those conditions, how on earth are they going to behave differently with your customers—especially if you're not around? If you get that "itchy" feeling that something's not quite right during the interview, take note. It will save you a lot of grief down the line.

■ HIRE WARM *PEOPLE,* NOT JUST "WARM BODIES"

It turned out I was right about Shamin (he goes by his last name) being a nice person. As a result, when he started work, everything he needed to be taught about the pizza business and about how I wanted my employees to treat customers came easily. In addition, he was passionate and wanted to learn. He became a popular deliveryman, and went out of his way to be friendly with everyone he met in his work. He got to know many of the doormen who work in the Upper East Side apartment buildings, and he was quick to take ownership of any customer concern because he wanted to make it right. It was not uncommon for many regular customers to request that Shamin deliver their pizzas to them. He did little things, like learning the names of customers' dogs and greeting them when they came to the door with their owners. Such small gestures made Shamin stand out.

Many business owners and managers who are hurting for employees take what they think is the easy way out: They hire whoever comes along. They may check to see if that person has a criminal record, but sometimes they don't. (You should, especially if your employees deliver to or provide a service at your customers' homes.) They may check references, but many times they don't. They may look closely enough at the application or may take things written on the application at face value without probing deeper. They may not take the time to properly interview a prospective employee. They may pay attention to those little items I listed previously, but often they don't. These are the easiest and best ways to make sure you don't make a hiring mistake right from the beginning! The hiring formula for many managers and business owners seems to be Warm Body = Job. That's not a good equation, as I learned in my first year on 89th Street. That's when I was faced with employees who mistreated customers, didn't take our standards seriously, and created such negative energy that I lost people I wish I could have kept on my team. By the time I got rid of the problem employees, I had to start from square one. Today, though, I'm in the business of hiring warm people who deliver hot pizzas!

Pay attention when you are out running errands, grocery shopping, buying pet food—anytime you are in the position of the customer. Notice how the customer service reps treat you. How do they make you feel? If you believe people genuinely like what they do and you think they would be good for your business, why not give them a business card and ask them to call you? I know a number of people who were offered job opportunities by Domino's franchisees because they delivered terrific service at their existing job.

You can get to the heart of a person's attitude with a few simple questions. I like to ask prospective employees to define what customer service means to them. I ask them how they would handle specific situations, especially customer complaints. I like to ask them how they would handle a customer complaint if they knew that the customer was "wrong." That will open your eyes! I've included an entire chapter on customer service later in this book and a list of tips my team devised for handling customer complaints, which we call, "Turning *Ow* into *Wow*."

■ FIX YOUR HIRING MISTAKES—FAST

In my first year, I was working 80 hours a week, trying to increase sales. In my haste to get my store staffed, I didn't make the kinds of hiring decisions I should have. I ended up with employees who thought it was easier to steal and be disruptive than to be part of a team and make an honest living. They would argue with customers, refuse to wear the uniform correctly, stop and visit their friends when they were supposed to be delivering to customers, and sometimes just not show up for work at all.

One of the biggest lessons I learned was, "Fix your hiring mistakes—fast."

At first I was hesitant to fire employees. No one likes to do it. But I came to realize that there are more honest people out there than dishonest ones, and I didn't have to settle for problem employees. The potential workforce in Manhattan is large, diverse, and growing. I was determined to take advantage of it!

If you're working in an area where the employment pool is more restricted, there are still some things you can do to find honest, pleasant people to hire. The first thing, of course, is to make sure that *you* are a pleasant person to work for! Managers who are brusque and intimidating will always have the toughest time hiring and retaining entry-level employees.

It's also important to pay competitively, especially when the labor pool is small. When I was just getting started, I would seek out my best, friendliest employees, and offer them a bonus if they could recruit other friendly people to apply for jobs at my shops. If I hired someone who was recruited by a team member, I would give both the recruiter and the new hire a bonus if the new employee stayed a minimum of 90 days.

In my shops, I also promote the fact that team members are free to enjoy a pizza "on the house" every once in a while. I want my team to enjoy one of the great side benefits of working at a pizza store . . . you get to eat pizza! And what better way to have your team become your number one reference? I've heard team members on the phone with customers saying things like, "My favorite pizza is the Deluxe. You should try that one!" I realize that not all businesses are in a position to offer their products for free to their employees, but surprising employees with special treats every once in a while creates a positive atmosphere, one that employees will talk about with their friends and families.

■ TURNING AROUND A TROUBLED WORK TEAM

When I decided to start investing more time in hiring and firing, I started by making it clear to everyone that there was greater upside—for all of us—if we could work on making great pizzas and becoming excellent at serving our customers. Everyone would be making more money, and nobody would have to resort to stealing a few bucks here and there. Most of my employees got it, although a few did not and they kept goofing off. I got rid of them.

However, I quickly found that, even when we were tight for employees, it wasn't the people that I fired that dragged me down . . . it was the ones we kept but *should* have let go that made me miserable! These problem employees were a distraction, and if you're like me you may be tempted to think that your problem employees are just another cost of doing business. If you're a manager or an owner, you know there are already plenty of these costs, and bad employees don't have to be one of them! It will be a real breakthrough for you when you realize that difficult employees can be somebody else's problem, not yours. My friend Mack Patterson, who owns several Domino's Pizza stores in North Carolina and is an inductee into the Chairman's Circle Hall of Fame, has a simple hiring philosophy, which he calls "No punks." I like that!

I came to realize that I was in this for the long haul, and I knew that whatever standards and examples I set in that first year were going to have an impact on my franchise for years to come. I ultimately learned that a little pain at the time of firing an employee and finding somebody new was always worth it when we improved the quality of the overall team. Even now, I always want my managers watching that bottom 10 percent of our employees and working on either improving them or replacing them. That way our team is always getting better.

If you are faced with problem employees, it is important to see if they can be salvaged before you let them go. Sometimes problem employees just need more training or need to be made aware that they are not performing up to your standards. You want to give them the benefit of the doubt. You'll find out fairly soon whether the issue is training or attitude. It's also helpful for you and the employee if you keep a record of your conversation and document the issues you are addressing. There are additional practical tips on this topic in Chapter 9.

■ HIRING WELL IS NOT JUST A TASK— IT'S AN *INVESTMENT* IN YOUR BUSINESS

Terminating problem employees had one immediate impact on me: I had to work longer and harder on hiring *well*—not just on hiring. I spent more time on recruiting and interviewing because I realized that this was the most important investment I was making in my franchise. (Yes, it was even more important than my life savings, which I used to get started!) My employees were the ones who were going to make the pizza and interact with my customers, so I had to get this part right. Once I began to think of hiring as an *investment*, I approached it differently.

Another impact on my business, one that took me a bit by surprise, was that overall store morale improved when I got rid of the thieves and malcontents. Honest people want to be around other honest people; friendly people want to be in an environment with other friendly people. I could almost hear a collective sigh of relief, a "thank goodness," from my team when I let the problem employees go. That freed up my good employees to excel at what they did best: making customers happy!

It also reinforced to everyone involved that I was serious about the messages I was sending. There is always some flexibility and leeway in any situation, and I believe in providing good people a second chance when they make mistakes, but there should always be lines that cannot be crossed without consequences. You absolutely cannot be rude to a customer—ever. You cannot be chronically late. And you cannot steal from me.

I knew the message was getting through in 1998 when my crew called me and asked me to fire a guy they said was ripping me off. He had been a manager for a fellow franchisee and was about to become a franchise owner himself.

There was going to be a lag of a few months between the end of his employment at his previous shop and the time he would open his own store for business. He asked me if he could work at my store during that lag. Of course, I agreed. I let him run the afternoon shift, handling the lunch business. It was only a few weeks later that I got the call from my team members, who said they had witnessed him taking carryout orders and collecting the money, but they never saw him actually enter the order into the computer, nor did they see him put the money in the till. It was all going directly into his pocket. He was brazenly stealing from me—while I was doing him a favor!

My crew couldn't take it and demanded that he be fired. I honored their wishes, and I thanked them for being so loyal and honest. In return, *they* thanked *me*. That one bad apple was bringing down morale, and all the other nice people I had hired were not happy that he was messing up the fun environment we had established—even though they were not directly affected by the theft. I had hired him, but my crew fired him. That's something I will never forget. (Incidentally, he failed as a franchise owner, not surprisingly, and left the system just a few months after opening his store. I can't say that we miss the guy.)

I've been in stores all over the country, and I can tell almost immediately whether the owner or manager has gotten hiring right—or wrong. If it's wrong, the energy level of the crew will be low; they'll appear disinterested and bored and look at customers as if they were a distraction instead of valuable people to take care of. It's odd, but just one bad hire can have a huge negative impact. If someone doesn't want to work for you, it's pretty easy to tell. It is amazing how just one person can raise the energy level in a store . . . and how one person can also bring it down.

A great store with positive people is brimming with energy—you can actually see it in the upbeat smiles of the employees and the speed with which they do their jobs, and that's exactly what you want. What you *don't* want is an atmosphere like the one in the TV show, *The Office*, where the employees spend their time in boring work, endlessly putting up with an overbearing boss. One of my favorite episodes is the one in which the employees of Dunder Mifflin compare their work environment to life in prison . . . and decide that prison sounds better!

➤ Problem Employees Are Worse Than You Think

Not all problem employees are thieves (at least, in the criminal sense), but in a way, they are. Problem employees steal the positive energy of your crew. They steal away the idea that we're all part of a team, and they create an "every person for him- or herself" attitude. That is exactly opposite of the ideal environment where the entire team benefits more because everyone is working together. Problem employees can drive away good ones, effectively robbing you of top performers. Ultimately, problem employees are going to drive away customers. Now, that's really stealing from you, even if they don't get any money in the process.

In our business, we cross-train and ask people to pitch in when and where needed. In slow times, for example, we ask our delivery team members to fold boxes in the back of the store or to help restock the pizza makeline. Sometimes we ask them to go out and hand out promotional fliers. When the store is busy, we ask them to answer the phone or take pizzas out of the oven, put them in boxes and assemble the order for delivery. The good team members will do that every time, without question. The problem employees will be the ones who insist that all they're paid to do is take pizzas from point A to point B, nothing else . . . and they will complain that they actually have to deal with *people* (meaning customers) in the process!

Not only do they not pitch in and help, putting more stress on the rest of the employees and creating animosity with their peers—they'll often harass or make fun of their teammates for doing what you ask of them, thereby creating even more animosity. If they will do that with people they see and interact with every day, just imagine how they'll behave with a customer they think they won't ever see again (and very likely won't)!

➤ Don't Hire Other People's Rejects: Check References

In the restaurant industry, where there is tremendous turnover, business owners tend to jump at hiring people with prior restaurant experience. More often than not, that's a good thing, but only if you check references. This is absolutely essential in the hospitality/customer service industry.

People leave employers in this industry for valid reasons all the time: because they're looking for better opportunities or more money; because they've graduated from school or are home for the summer; any number of reasons. I'm not suggesting you hire only inexperienced team members, but if you do hire someone who has worked someplace else, do yourself the favor of making that five-minute phone call to his or her previous employer(s). You might be surprised at the things you'll learn.

At Domino's Pizza, I know many franchisees who are extremely eager to hire delivery drivers or store managers who have had previous Domino's experience and never once think to call their previous employer. That absolutely blows my mind, because we're not competitors—we're franchisees with the *same company*! Not only could they learn why or why not to hire an individual, they'd also be making a connection with a peer—someone who knows exactly the kinds of challenges they're facing and who could (and happily would) help them out with some advice or guidance. Instead, when they see "Domino's Pizza" on the application, they hire the applicant, no questions asked. That's asking for trouble. Domino's has thousands of great employees, but, as with every organization, we have a few bad apples. Your industry probably does, too. You have enough to deal with as a manager or an owner of a business without taking on somebody else's rejects while you're at it. Let your competitors do that!

Checking references is perhaps the simplest way to determine whether an applicant is worth a second look. It's also a great opportunity to get to know someone else—someone who might become a new customer of yours, a peer who can share ideas with you, or even a new employee!

➤ Hire People with Entrepreneurial Spirit

Zia Shah, who was born in Pakistan, and holds a business degree, has been working in my franchise for more than a decade. His goal is to one day own his own Domino's Pizza franchise. In his home country, "Everyone has a dream to come to America," he says. "Dreams come true for everybody here."

Zia likes to tell his story. He arrived in the United States alone, in 1998. He had no connections in New York, but had an uncle who lived in Houston. The uncle had a friend in New York who happened to know one of my store managers and offered to put Zia in touch with him. Days later, Zia was applying for a job. He started at minimum wage and worked as a delivery employee for 18 months, but he wanted more. "During that time, my manager taught me how to make pizza and how to answer the phone to take orders from our customers," he says. "One day I was feeling frustrated. Then I saw my franchisee wearing a Rolex watch that he won in a sales competition as a manager. I wanted one, so I decided I had to become a store manager." Zia started to shadow his store manager, watching how he interacted with customers, how he drafted the weekly schedule, how he ordered food from the supply chain center, and how he completed the weekly paperwork. He asked to run shifts in the manager's absence to get hands-on experience. That's the kind of self-starter I was looking for and the entrepreneurial spirit I love. "When I franchise, I will be the first person in my family to own a business," Zia says, proudly.

On his way to becoming a manager, I encouraged Zia every time I visited the store. I'd quiz him on the kinds of things a store manager was responsible for and offer him positive feedback on his work. I also promised him that when he was ready and there was a position available, he would be a manager. Now he's been a store manager since 2005 . . . and he's earned not one, but two custom Rolex watches, featuring the Domino's Pizza logo on its face, by achieving sales of more than $20,000 and $25,000 a week, respectively, for four consecutive weeks—not an easy thing to do! He did it by aggressively promoting sales, but more important, by impressing every customer and motivating his crew constantly. Zia sent one Rolex to his father and the second to his mother back home in Pakistan. Zia was also named the Manager of the Year for Domino's Pizza New York in 2007.

You can find people with this kind of entrepreneurial spirit almost anywhere. They are the ones who ask a lot of questions of business owners to learn as much as they can. They are the ones who have an extra energy when it comes to making it big. They have an idea and a fire in their bellies to own their own business. They may be entry-level employees looking for experience and money to get them started, or they may be in a job that is unfulfilling and want to work for themselves doing something they love to do. Entrepreneurs are passionate.

Here's another great entrepreneurial story. Jim Denburg walked past my Domino's Pizza store on 89th Street in New York every day on the way to his job as a certified public accountant for Price Waterhouse in the early 1990s. Although he was successful by many people's standards, working in one of the major global accounting firms, he was bored with his job and yearned for something different, like owning his own business. He had done his research, and knew that Domino's Pizza was a growing franchise company. One day, he finally came in and mentioned that he kept seeing all of this energy and excitement in the store and he had to know more about my experience with Domino's. When I explained to him who I was and how I came to be the owner of the store, Jim was intrigued. He wanted to become a part of it. I insisted that the only way he could truly decide was for him to become a part of our team, and that way he could see our business from the inside.

He wanted to learn everything he could before making that leap and joining me in the ranks of Domino's Pizza franchisees. The first thing I had him do was deliver pizzas for a couple of months. He loved it! Soon, after talking it over with his family, Jim quit his job at the firm and became an assistant manager at one of my stores. After a year as a store manager, he became a franchisee. Today, Jim is a friend and not only owns a wildly successful store in New York City (his manager, Jesús Arriaga, was named the Domino's Pizza U.S. Manager of the Year two years in a row), but also owns successful Domino's stores in Amsterdam, Holland, and commutes back and forth to Europe every few months. How's that for a former CPA with a boring accounting job?

➤ Happy Employees Are Your Best Recruiters

These days, my best and happiest employees are also my best recruiters. Because they're having a great time on the job and are being successful, they want others to join them. I actively encourage my best employees to recruit their friends. Many business owners shy away from that because they think friends will goof off more or figure out a way to cheat them. In my experience, it's just the opposite—they will only recruit the friends they know who will fit in and work hard. Anyone an employee recruits essentially becomes an extension of that employee and will definitely have an impact on the employee's reputation and credibility. For many of the team members who work in my stores, who come from Bangladesh, the African nation of Burkina Faso, Mexico, Puerto Rico, and other cultures, pride, reputation, and credibility are extremely important. They are not going to give those things away by recommending someone unless they are absolutely sure that person "deserves" to work for "our" pizza store. Imagine that!

When I was just starting out, I provided incentives for team members to recruit others because I desperately needed the staffing. Today, I don't have to, because my team is stable and they're looking for great candidates to join us on their own. We even have a waiting list of people who hope to join our team when we have an opening!

You can benefit by encouraging your best employees to recruit family and friends. Sweeten the pot and offer a recruiting bonus of some kind if the new hire stays for a minimum of 90 days. I've seen younger employees even recruiting their parents!

➤ Use Your Experienced Employees to Interview Prospective Hires

Another important thing I do is insist that the manager in my store is not the only one who conducts job interviews. Someone on the same level as the applicant also conducts an interview with the prospective hire. That way, the prospective employee gets a real picture of the job and meets a potential peer (and possible future friend), and the interviewing employee can provide crucial feedback on whether the applicant has the right stuff for the job. This makes the transition into the job easier for new employees, because they've already made a connection with a seasoned employee who can show them how to do the job more effectively and who can introduce them to other employees in the store. It also is a proven morale booster for the existing employee, who appreciates that he or she has been entrusted with such an important role in determining who works in the store. Try this in your business. You'll find that your employees will appreciate the trust you've shown in them, and it will take a bit of the burden of hiring off of you, because you will benefit from another person's perspective.

Because I learned, through a lot of trial and error, that it's better to hire for attitude than for skill (I can teach people the pizza business, but I can't truly teach them character), I've been able to focus my hiring efforts on hiring *nice*.

Which brings me back to Shaik Shamin, who walked into my pizza store in 1996. We hired him because it was obvious that he was an eager learner, wanted to succeed, wanted to make an impression, and was just plain nice. When he became a manager, I knew that the store was in good hands. He had worked hard to learn how to manage a pizza store, and he already had a great reputation for taking care of customers from his days as a deliveryman. With Shamin at the helm, sales in the store continued to improve, and customer concerns continued to drop. With Shamin, "nice" is a natural state of being.

Shamin managed the store on 32nd Street when the tragic events of September 11, 2001, unfolded in New York City. Shamin made his way to the store that morning, walking nearly 100 blocks because he knew we were going to have to help get food to people in need. He worked at the store for several consecutive days with a team of volunteers to feed rescue workers, police officers, firefighters, and people displaced by the tragedy. (A profile of Shamin and more on the events of September 11 appear later in the book.)

A few years ago, Domino's Pizza, Inc., chairman of the board and chief executive officer David Brandon was speaking at one our big franchise conventions, called the Worldwide Rally. Dave stood before the assembled throng of more than 3,500 people and declared, "We've conducted countless hours of market research over the years, and we've spoken to literally tens of thousands of customers and here's what we've learned: People call us when they're hungry. Hungry people want to be fed *now*. If we can deliver great pizzas *fast* and be *nice* about it when we do it, there's nothing that can get in our way."

Thus, for some time, "Fast and Nice" became a mantra for our brand. Deliver pizzas fast and be nice to people when we do it. How much simpler can it get? The company was so caught up in this rallying cry of *Fast and Nice* that the corporation created an award category around it. The Fast and Nice Manager of the Year award would be presented at the Worldwide Rally to the store general manager whose store was among the best at "fast" (in our business, this means how quickly pizzas are made and how quickly they are out the door on the way to customers) and the best at "nice" (based on customer comments and/or nominations from their franchisee or supervisor and other internal measures).

The winner receives a plaque and international recognition in our company, and the first-year award included a VIP trip for two to a NASCAR race, which included a chance to meet drivers on the Domino's Pizza NASCAR team that year and a tour of the pit area. The winner of the first-ever Domino's Pizza Fast and Nice Manager of the Year Award: Shaik Shamin.

AMERICAN DREAM EMPLOYEE: ZAKIR SHAFI

From Winning Immigrant Lottery to Living the American Dream

Zakir Shafi didn't have the chance to finish high school. That hasn't stopped him from living his dream. In 1995, when he was 17 and attending his final year of secondary school in Bangladesh, Zakir's mother entered the immigrant lottery for a chance to obtain a visa to emigrate to the United States. She won the lottery, and before Zakir could finish school, he and his immediate family, five people in all, landed in New York—with just $200 between them.

"We just wanted to see what America was like. We didn't know if we were going to stay," he says. "Much of our family that is no longer in Bangladesh is in Toronto. We didn't know where we would end up." The family moved into a small apartment with other Bengalis in the Bronx, and Zakir immediately began looking for work to support them. Within days, he landed a job delivering sandwiches for a small deli, and in the first week, thanks to his paycheck and tips, he doubled the family's money. They decided to stay.

Things were going well, but Zakir wanted more. "I made all of my deliveries on foot and I kept noticing all these Domino's delivery guys going past me on bikes. I stopped one of the delivery guys and started talking to him. He encouraged me to come to Domino's. I got a job delivering pizzas for the 74th Street store in 1996, and I was making $70 to $80 a night in tips. I couldn't believe it. I made $150 in tips on Christmas Day." He was hooked.

After 18 months, Zakir began asking about management opportunities. "I knew that I would be making less money as an assistant manager, because there are no tips, but to get something, you have to give. So, I made a little less money, but I wanted to learn. I wanted to be a general manager." Like a sponge, he began absorbing everything he could about store management. "I learned a lot from my manager—good stuff and bad stuff. I asked a lot of questions. I made him crazy with my questions. The best advice I got was to never say no to a customer. You've got to always make the customers happy."

One of the things that motivated Zakir toward management was that he wanted to see himself literally move up on the list of employees at the store. On the weekly schedule, the manager's name is at the top, followed by the assistant manager, crew chief, and so on down to the newest, entry-level person—where Zakir's name was. That visual reference kept him focused week in and week out. "I started at the bottom of the list and I worked to make my way to the top of the list," he says proudly.

What keeps him motivated after more than 12 years in the pizza delivery business? "It is very hard to find a very good job like this without a high school education in this country," Zakir says. "Dave gives us the opportunity to run his stores, and we owe it to him to be faithful. Domino's is like our family."

From 1999 to 2005, Zakir managed the store on 74th Street. He loved delighting customers. Following up on an idea inspired by his previous manager, Zakir liked to surprise new customers when they walked into his store by telling them they just won the "New Customer" prize and that they could pick the price they would pay for their order, no strings attached. Not once did anyone say they wanted the pizza free, which surprised him, but the gesture always generated smiles from the customers, who made it a point to come back. Zakir did such a great job, he was a nominee for regional manager of the year for the Northeast.

In 2003, Zakir got married and saw his years of hard work and saving money pay off, as he purchased his first car and his first home. He was indeed living the American Dream. He is also helping his younger brother prepare to go to college, an opportunity Zakir didn't have but does not regret.

"I like challenges. I keep saying, 'Give me something new.' I love to learn and I'm going to keep learning until I become a franchisee some day. I want to own my own business, but until then, I work for Dave. I get lots of job offers from other pizza places. Papa John's used to bother me with job offers. I asked them to stop calling me. Dave helped change me. When I started, I was very shy and he paid the bill to send me to the Dale Carnegie course. I learned a lot from that. I was shy, but now I'm comfortable talking to anyone. Dave did that for me."

Today Zakir has taken the reins of a couple of new stores that Dave and Angie have acquired outside of the city. He relishes the challenge of managing a store in which deliveries

(Continued)

(Continued)

are made by car, not by bicycle. "The business is much different outside the city, but the stores are in great markets and I'm putting together great teams. I'm going to learn as much as I can as fast as possible.

"I love this business," Zakir continues. "I think about it all the time. I only go to sleep when I know the stores are closed, and I make sure I'm awake all the time they're open. I just want to be available if they need me. Sometimes at home, I accidentally answer the phone, 'Domino's Pizza,' I think about it so much. Because of Domino's, I have a house and a car in this country. I am married and my wife inspires me. It is like a dream coming true for me."

Chapter 3

Recent Immigrants Have Much to Offer

The face of the American entry-level workforce is changing. Throughout the nation, frontline employees who will work for minimum wages are increasingly coming from the immigrant population, especially in densely populated urban markets such as New York City, Atlanta, Miami, Houston, and Los Angeles. Many of my employees come from Mexico, Puerto Rico, the Dominican Republic, Pakistan, Bangladesh, and Burkina Faso. Census bureau estimates show that 8 million immigrants arrived in the United States between 2000 and 2007. (Census estimates show that two-thirds of those 8 million recent arrivals went to the South and the West regions.)

In New York City, the diverse nature of the city can be experienced simply by hailing a taxi cab or two or visiting a newspaper stand. The minimum-wage labor pool in New York is extremely large—and it's mostly from immigrant communities. This is certainly true in my stores.

Some people think that just because a person is struggling with the language, they are somehow less intelligent or less educated. That is, unfortunately, a common misconception I've heard from others about the members of my team and about immigrants in general. The team members at my stores are smart, they're here legally, the majority of them are now citizens of the United States, all of them are taxpay-ers, and most of them are hard workers like I am. They're also great human beings once you learn to see past the sur-face differences that sometimes prejudice us.

I've found it incredibly enlightening and rewarding to learn about other cultures and see employees from all over the world interact with each other in my stores in New York City. I've discovered that people are much more similar than they appear at first. It's wonderful to see Muslims, Jews, and Christians happily working together. I find they are kind, loving, spiritual people, who are raising their families and contributing to the fabric of our society, but who sometimes have to struggle with the stereotypes thrust upon them by suspicious fellow citizens.

The team members who work in my stores are not afraid of hard work, because they know it leads to something—more money. They also have fun, because there is little in the busi-ness world that can get your juices flowing like being in a pizza store in the middle of a rush—making 150 or 200 pies an hour. The energy and excitement of taking the orders, mak-ing each pizza correctly, getting them in the right boxes, and getting them out the door with everything else the customer ordered (breadsticks, chicken wings, soft drinks)—and doing it all in 10 minutes per order—is very difficult to describe. As with an athletic event, to do that week in and week out takes real passion. What a thrill it is to be a part of a highly trained team, expertly handling the rush!

Immigrants are often great employees because they come to this country seeking the American Dream, and they expect to actively participate in the American work ethic. They hear of the "Land of Opportunity" and are anxious to get to work and to assimilate. In my experience, they are also "clean slates," ready to be taught the American work ethic, cul-ture, and values. Most entry-level employees are looking for experience, opportunity, and, of course, money. Immigrants are also looking to learn how to best function in American culture. Sometimes business owners and managers fall into the trap of "hiring themselves," meaning they hire only people who look like them, have the same background, and maybe went to the same high school or college. That's fine, but it eliminates a tremendous number of potential workers for their businesses. If savvy business owners are willing to work with immigrants and support them, they will be rewarded with years of loyal service and great performance from their employees.

■ LOWER WAGES DO NOT MEAN LOWER-QUALITY WORK OR LOWER-QUALITY WORKERS

It is a common misperception that if you pay an employee (foreign-born or otherwise) the minimum wage, all you're going to get is minimum quality. I totally disagree. The minimum wage would be better described as the "starting wage," because those who tackle the job at hand and do good work for their employer are going to end up making more money. The starting wage allows teenagers to get their first job experience, for example, and allows employers the chance to create those entry-level job opportunities.

Minimum-wage positions also allow entry-level workers who are new to the country a way to begin assimilating into American culture. The only people, in my opinion, who are forever stuck in minimum wage jobs with no hope for an increase probably work for very bad bosses (who will likely never read *this* book!), bosses who make their profits on the backs of their workers and who don't believe in sharing success with them. Virtually every one of my employees has started at the minimum wage, and all of them now make more . . . in many cases, much more!

Immigrant workers, I've found, don't come with the same kinds of attitudes about entry-level work that some Americans have. Immigrant workers appreciate the opportunity and don't bring a "me first" or entitlement attitude to the job. They don't easily dismiss burger-flipping or pizza-tossing jobs as dead-end jobs . . . in fact, they see them for what they are (especially at Domino's): opportunities to start on the ground floor of a successful global enterprise leading to management and business ownership opportunities. All of the work experience a new employee gets at Domino's—experience in teamwork, hustle, leadership, customer relations, and hard work—could easily transfer to nearly any career. What Fortune 500 company doesn't want those attributes in its employees? At Domino's Pizza in the United States today, there are more than 1,200 independent franchisees just like me. The average Domino's franchisee owns three stores, employing anywhere from 30 to 50 people. More than 1,000 of those business owners started as pizza delivery drivers.

■ TEACH FAIRNESS AND THE IMPORTANCE OF STANDARDS

Just because many of my team members are hourly workers or are learning English as a second language, I don't lower my standards of performance, nor do I lower my expectations for my team. (My friend Jeff Litman, who owns Domino's Pizza stores around Lakewood, Colorado, reminds me that you never need to apologize for having high standards.) Everyone, no matter how new he or she is, is trained from the beginning about the expectations and the culture of my franchise. You wouldn't drive through a stop sign, would you? Of course you wouldn't. It's too dangerous. That's the way I feel about the standards I set for my operations. I find that being fair, consistent, and predictable is an easy way to get what I want! Make your standards and policies absolutely clear. Everyone should know the expectations and should also know what happens when they don't meet those expectations. That way it's not a surprise when an employee is reprimanded for a policy violation. In fact, on my teams, they typically already know what the penalty will be if they don't follow a standard.

I never let a standards violation go past me without commenting on it. All my employees are required to have a name tag on their uniform, for example, and if they "forget" their tag, I'm happy to sell them a new one for a dollar. Eventually (it usually doesn't take very long), they'll stop forgetting to bring their name tag to work. If people violate some of my other standards, they always seem to be the ones who are "volunteered" for unpleasant jobs in the store, like cleaning the grease traps or mopping the restroom. I'm also a fanatic about making sure that the phones in my stores are answered by the second ring, and preferably after only one ring. That's been ingrained in me—so much so that I find myself practically freaking out at friends' houses when they let their own phones ring more than twice; I struggle not to answer their phone myself!

Here's a quick aside about the attitudes of some American-born workers. In 2008, Domino's Pizza introduced an innovative piece of technology called Pizza Tracker, which allows customers to go online at www.dominos.com and, by entering the phone number used to order, "track" where their pizza is at every step in the process, from the makeline to the oven to their door. Customers can even see the first name of the delivery person who will be knocking on their door. Inside the store, it's seamless and adds no extra work for Domino's employees, because Pizza Tracker is directly tied into the store's computer system. It's a phenomenal tool, and our customers really love it. Most of our employees do, too. So I was a bit shocked and surprised to see a comment from an anonymous Domino's employee about Pizza Tracker, written on an internal company discussion board.

I'm paraphrasing, but the employee's point was that allowing customers to track their order puts pressure on the store crew, and "true Americans" don't want to work that hard! In fact, he says, the impact is that if companies are looking for people to work hard, they end up hiring "illegal immigrants, which promotes anti-American values . . . and ends up putting true Americans out of jobs because they aren't willing to do extra work."

The idea that "true" Americans don't like to work hard astounds me (and I honestly believe he was speaking only for himself, not for other American workers), but the idea that people who *do* work hard must be illegal immigrants is ludicrous! My two cents: This guy is the "problem employee" at his store, and he is bringing the energy level and customer service in that store down, down, down. He needs to go.

■ PASSION IS MORE IMPORTANT THAN SKILL

As I said in the previous chapter, I will hire *attitude* over *experience* every time. Likewise, I also prefer *passion* over *skill*. Order taking and pizza making I can teach (so can my store managers); passion I can *fuel*, but it's got to be there in the first place. Zia Shah was initially fueled by the passion to win a Rolex watch. Now he's fueled by the goal of owning his own pizza franchise one day. I am here to support him in that quest, because even though we were born in different countries and into different circumstances, we are quite alike in more than a few ways.

When Zia came to New York City on his own from Pakistan, he was a stranger in a strange land. There is nothing in Pakistan that rivals the Big Apple. But you know what? There's nothing in Virginia, where I came from, like New York City, either. I felt like a stranger in a strange land when I arrived in Manhattan in the late 1980s. I had to make my way around, confronting myriad challenges and situations I had never faced back home. So I can appreciate, to some degree, what it is like to be in a new and overwhelming place.

Zia and I also both hold business degrees. From different universities on different continents, to be sure, but both of us sought a higher education and pursued degrees in business management. But where he and I are most alike is this: We are entrepreneurs and we have a passion for the pizza business, for ownership, and for living the American Dream. We are both competitive and love sports. We love to win. That connects us and drives us both.

For so many immigrants to America, the United States truly is the land of opportunity, for it provides them with a place to earn a living, to raise their children, and to pursue their dreams, especially if managers and owners will give them the chance, like I have. They are not the only ones who have been rewarded: So have I. It was difficult for them to leave their homelands, but today they call America home. Opportunities in their homelands are limited; in America, they are limitless. I'm proud to be a part of it.

Chapter 4

Teach Philosophy and Opportunity First

In my more than 25 years at Domino's, I think I have found one of the true secrets to success for a business owner, and it's this:

Make your vision "contagious."

As the owner of the business, one of my most important jobs is to share my vision with my employees and make it contagious. The vision for my business is busy pizza stores—phones ringing, ovens full, people hustling—filled with enthusiastic team members committed to making customers happy . . . and being rewarded for it. This is my vision, and my employees know it and for the most part share it, because they've heard me talk about it with enthusiasm so frequently. You have a vision for your business. What is it? If your employees don't know what it is, how can they help you get there? Do they know what role they play? Do they know what's in it for them when you achieve your goals? Do they know how passionate you are about it? Let your team know that you want your company to be the best at whatever it is you do. Define for them what "best" means, who you're competing against, and how to be the best.

When I joined the company, the companywide Domino's Pizza Mission was simple: *to safely deliver a hot, quality pizza in 30 minutes or less, guaranteed.* It was easy to understand, easy to communicate, and everything we did focused our attention on that mission. We eventually had to drop the guarantee due to misperceptions that we encouraged our delivery drivers to behave unsafely in the course of their jobs. (We didn't, but that's a discussion for another book.) Now the Domino's Pizza Vision reads: *Exceptional franchisees and team members on a mission to be the best pizza delivery company in the world.* There is power in the words *exceptional* and *best.* Who doesn't want to be identified by that description?

But "missions" and "visions" are not the first thing on the minds of minimum-wage, entry-level employees. When I ask a potential new hire what his or her "mission" is, I usually get the same answer: "to make money." Actually, that's a pretty good place to start! Knowing that making money is their initial goal, I can provide them with a lot of information about how to make more of it.

■ SHARE YOUR VISION OF SUCCESS

With entry-level hourly employees, I may ask about their mission in a more informal way, but no less directly: "Why are you here?" Surely, I suggest, they can't be working for Domino's because they like wearing the uniform (although they are cool uniforms) or because they like riding their bike through the Manhattan streets at night in the rain or the snow. They can't be working here because they aspire to be a pizza delivery guy or gal . . . or can they?

I didn't go to college to be a pizza delivery guy. But what happened to me is that I discovered an opportunity in which I could make more money, almost immediately, based on how good of a job I did. The better I performed, the more money I would make. Eventually, I realized I could turn that entry-level job into an opportunity to own my own business. What was special about Domino's Pizza (and still is today) is that the company's preferred franchisee was someone who started near the bottom and came up through the system. For the longest time, the only way to become eligible to franchise at Domino's was to be a successful store manager for a minimum of one year. The franchise fee is among the lowest in the quick-service restaurant industry, and because Domino's is primarily a delivery company, the stores themselves don't need much in the way of square footage, which helps keep rent down. The typical Domino's Pizza store costs are low in comparison to other chains (between $175,000 and $250,000). In addition, because typical franchise candidates have already managed a store for at least a year, they know what kind of business they're getting into.

Tom Monaghan, the founder of the company, said that he developed this "long engagement" philosophy before franchising because he thought franchising should be like a great marriage, one that lasted a long, long time. The business model was simple: Treat customers well, make great pizzas, and deliver them quickly. It's a job that lets you know *as you're doing it* whether you are succeeding. Add in a low cost of entry, plus the ability to own your own business in just a few short years—this was the path to the American Dream for me.

Most entry-level employees approach a new job looking to make some money and gain some experience before moving on to something else. They don't necessarily think of that initial job as a platform from which to build a career. But that is exactly my message: Entry-level employees truly *can* start here and work their way into store management, into a job with the corporation in the United States or internationally, or they could end up owning their own store. You don't necessarily need a college degree to make it here.

In a 2008 newspaper article, a reporter interviewed Scott Hinshaw, Domino's executive vice president of franchise operations and development. Scott started working for $4.50 an hour at a Domino's shop in suburban Chicago in the early 1980s and is now reporting directly to the president of Domino's USA. He's responsible for working with 1,200 Domino's franchisees across the country. The reporter asked Scott to define the most important lesson he's learned in 20 years of business management. Scott's answer:

"You don't need an MBA to do a good J-O-B."

Patti Wilmot, executive vice president of PeopleFirst at Domino's, says the toughest thing to communicate to hourly employees is that there is *career* potential in the company they're working for. Not all hourly entry-level jobs need to be short-term or dead-end jobs; they certainly aren't at Domino's!

With my fellow franchisees and supervisors of the company-owned stores in the greater New York area, we periodically conduct what we call "manager rallies." It's important to get peers together, especially those in the same market with the same challenges, to share lessons and best practices. At these rallies, we seek out and invite high-profile executives in the company or successful franchisees to speak to the managers. Hearing their stories reminds the managers that these highly-successful individuals started out just like them. I love to expose my team members to other successful entrepreneurs. They learn new things and they stay excited about the opportunities that lie before them.

I tell my delivery people who are ambitious about a guy named Stan Gage. Stan was born and raised in Cleveland, Ohio. When he was old enough, Stan joined the military. When he got out, his options seemed limited. Then he began delivering pizzas for Domino's in Cleveland. After a few years, Stan realized there was more opportunity here than just earning an hourly wage and tips. He became a store manager. But instead of pursuing franchising, Stan moved his way up through the corporation, taking a number of highly responsible positions: He lived in Europe and helped develop new franchises there; he came back to the United States to become a regional vice president, working with franchisees throughout the Midwest. He is now vice president of training. His story is really not unique. There are hundreds and hundreds of these success stories throughout Domino's, and some of them are the team members who work for me in Manhattan.

And on the way up, I remind my employees, the more pizza you sell along the way, the more money you're going to make.

This is true even of the hourly employees who deliver pizzas in my stores. I tell my delivery employees that their job is not only to *deliver* pizza but to help *sell* pizza. What's in it for them? Plenty—the more pizzas we sell, the more addresses they deliver to, which means more potential opportunities for tips. Tips are cash in their pockets, cash they can take home that very night. They don't have to wait until payday. And when a store does well (meaning it sells a lot of pizza), Angie and I celebrate by distributing bonuses—more money in their pockets. Instead of complaining that all they're paid to do is take a box from point A to point B, my delivery team members actively promote the product every chance they get!

■ THINK LIKE A COACH AND FIND WAYS TO FIRE UP YOUR TEAM

As a business owner, I believe I am responsible for providing four crucial things to everyone who works for me: *motivation, inspiration, education,* and *compensation.* As a manager or owner, these are your responsibilities, too. Let's take a look at these in more detail.

➤ Motivation

I approach my job as a coach would. I constantly try to fire up my team to perform today better than they did yesterday. If they can sell just a few more pizzas today and a few more than that tomorrow, sales will continually go up, I tell them. When sales go up, everybody wins. I believe in positive-energy motivation, not negative-energy intimidation.

I use simple techniques like the "fist bump" (that's the hipper version of the classic "high five") with a person who's done a great job. No matter what part of the world my employees are from, the fist bump translates. It is universally understood! I love to boost the energy level in my stores, and my team gets pumped up, especially on very busy nights, by cheering them on, by giving them coaching and positive reinforcement when they're getting it right and they're hustling.

My team loves it when customers visiting the store comment on how fast they're moving and how much fun they seem to be having. That makes them move faster and have even more fun doing it. A busy store keeps you in shape, because consecutive hundred-pie hours take energy, skill, and endurance—like an athletic event. We get pumped up and excited for some very busy nights throughout the year: New Year's Eve, which is *big* in Manhattan; Super Bowl Sunday (the biggest day for pizza sales in the United States); and, here in New York City, any night it rains! New Yorkers hate rain; Domino's Pizza stores love it. People don't want to go out, so they order in. Raindrops are like pennies from heaven. The team has to stay motivated to make it through those very busy times.

➤ Inspiration

I like to tell inspirational stories to my team to show them that there is no shame to working in a pizza shop. In fact, there can be a lot of pride in it. Sometimes I tell my employees about individuals who started as delivery people (just like them) and became millionaire business owners (just like me).

Sometimes I tell them simple stories, like the one about Barry Jessen, a man who delivered pizza for Domino's in Salt Lake City, Utah, for over 18 years. Barry loved his job and was very good at it. He had the knack for great customer service. Whenever Barry was delivering to a house and saw the newspaper in the yard, he would pick it up and put it in his delivery bag. When he got to the front door, he would announce to the customer, "I've got some hot news for you to go along with your hot pizza." Silly, maybe, but his customers loved it. Service like that made Barry stand out, as did this: One day Barry was delivering to a house located up on a mountain. During the drive, his car got hopelessly stuck in the snow, so Barry did what he had to do—delivered the pizza by trekking the rest of the way up the mountain on foot! Barry was in his fifties at the time. Today, Barry is general manager of that Salt Lake City store.

➤ Education

Training and education are critical in minimum-wage jobs. My store managers and I work every day to ensure that people learn and understand the basics of great customer service, how to make pizzas better and faster than anyone else, and how to make a positive impact on the community and, in turn, increase sales. At my manager meetings, I usually open with a question about store operations or customer service, such as, "What are the five things you must absolutely do on the phone?" There's no prize for the person answering correctly, other than the pride in knowing he or she got it right—but more important, it's a good reminder of what they should be doing on every phone call. In case you're wondering, the five must-do phone items are as follows: (1) Give an enthusiastic, branded greeting: "Thank you for calling Domino's Pizza!"

(2) Repeat the order back to the customer to ensure we got it right. (3) Take the opportunity to ask if customers would like to add a beverage or a side item to their order. (4) Remind them that they have 30 minutes before the order will arrive. (5) Sincerely thank them for their business.

➤ Compensation

Compensation is what brings applicants in the door, of course: They want to earn money. In the highly competitive restaurant industry, in a bustling city like New York, compensation has to be competitive. That's what we offer: a competitive wage with the opportunity to earn tips every night in an environment that's energetic, fun, and filled with opportunity.

My managers share in the profits of the stores they are responsible for. When one of our stores has a particularly good sales month, Angie and I make sure every team member shares in the success. I always tell my team that I would much rather pay $1,000 in bonuses than $1,000 in equipment repairs or health department fines. My employees prefer that, too, especially because I charge the cost of repairs or fines against the store's bottom line, which negatively impacts the store's profitability and thus the manager's compensation. Bonuses, however, come directly from Angie and me. I believe in rewarding my employees, because without them, I wouldn't be successful, and they know that (because I tell them, often!).

■ MAKE SURE EVERYBODY WINS

If you run your business right, everyone can win, especially if you focus on the right order of priority. For me, it's (1) *customer,* (2) *team member,* (3) *owner* (or *manager*).

Customers come first because they are the boss. Our customers decide whether we are going to be open for business tomorrow and the next day. Customers have to believe that they get a great meal and terrific service at a price they feel is of real value. Value doesn't mean "cheap," it means that they get what they pay for—and a bit more. My objective is not to have merely satisfied customers; I want *delighted* customers. Those are the ones who will keep coming back. That's why, at the very least, I have the *Absolutely, Positively Cannot Be Rude to a Customer—Ever* rule. Violate that, and you're seeking employment opportunities elsewhere.

My team members are crucial to making customers happy. Good bosses know that their people have a significant impact on their success. If your employees don't want you to succeed, you won't. The way to make them want you to succeed is to address their needs and to make them happy. When I make my team members happy through motivation, inspiration, education, and compensation, they'll go out of their way to make customers happy. That ultimately leads to the win-win-win result: Happy customers and happy team members make the business owner happy! In the end, if you treat your team members like they are number one, you won't have to worry about how they're treating your customers.

Patti Wilmot says, "The biggest mistake hiring managers make when working with hourly workers is thinking the employees check their brains at the door when they come to work. They don't, unless you continue to treat them that way. We all want to be respected, to be heard, to know that our ideas and suggestions have merit." If you can engage employees and involve their ideas in the operations of the business, you'd be amazed at the talent you'll discover.

➤ Reinforce Key Messages Until Your Employees Can Repeat Them Back to You

With entry-level employees (and even with your managers), it's important to repeat your key messages, no matter how crazy you might make your team members. In his autobiography, *Pizza Tiger*, Domino's Pizza founder Tom Monaghan talks about his repeated messages regarding making great pizzas and providing exceptional service:

> *I kept harping on these things (product quality and thirty-minute service) at every meeting we had. My employees might moan and groan at hearing me repeat them, but I didn't let that bother me. It isn't enough to know what you want: You have to make sure that the people who can get it for you know you want it. You'll know they know when they start saying it back to you. If you show them you want it enough, they'll know it, too—and when they do, they'll get it for you.*

That's why I open my meetings with questions like, "How many pepperoni are there on a large pizza?" and "What kind of customers do we want?" Those things are important to me and cannot be reinforced enough. (The answers to those last questions are "48" and "customers for *life*.")

Other things I harp on (to use Tom's phrase) are, "Always answer the phone within two rings," and "Never put a person on hold." Those are critical to exceptional customer service. Here's why: Customers do not know or care how busy you are; they only care how hungry *they* are. When you go to any restaurant, you know when you walk in the door (sometimes even before) how busy it is, based on the number of people waiting around or sitting at the bar. The host or hostess will clearly tell you that you could wait 45 minutes to an hour just to get a table. And many of us accept that without argument.

But when you're on the phone at Domino's or are ordering online, you automatically think of yourself as "first in line." Our job is to help make you think and believe that you *are* first in line! We know that you don't care if there are

20 orders in front of you. We have to make sure that we make your order and get it to you as quickly as possible. If we let the phone ring too long or if we put you on hold before you can even say a word, we're unintentionally sending you a message that someone is in front of you or that you're not important to us. We try to never let that happen.

➤ Use the Tools Available to You to Manage What's Important

At Domino's Pizza stores worldwide, our computers have many features that track performance. We're extremely time-oriented, because our customers are time-oriented. Time moves awfully slowly when someone is waiting for food to arrive, so we fanatically keep track of how fast we can get custom made pizzas into the oven (our goal is less than three minutes from the time you hang up the phone) and how quickly we can have a delivery person headed out the door with your order (the goal at my stores is to do that within 10 minutes from the time you hang up or click the "Submit order" button on your computer). These measurements help us identify possible bottlenecks in our operations or find better ways to plan our store floor designs or ways to improve our pizza-making process. We call this fanatical timing of everything "Heightened Time Awareness," or HTA, because so much of what we do revolves around getting pizzas made quickly and out the door to our customers in as little time as possible.

Our emphasis on HTA is meant to help lessen the rapid drop-off in what we call our customers' "emotional roller coaster." It's a pretty interesting concept, coined after research and conversations with thousands of customers. Here's what we've learned: During the pizza-ordering process, people's emotional highs come in two places—first, when they make the decision to order a pizza and, second, when it arrives. Those are the two big hills of the coaster. The big emotional dip? That comes immediately after they've hung up the phone or clicked the "Submit order" button. Because they're not sitting in a restaurant, where their server can refill their water glass and let them know their meal is coming up, our customers have to wait and hope that we got it right and that we're on the way. That's the primary reason we developed the Web-based Pizza Tracker, which I talked about in Chapter 3. Before that, the only way we could prevent that emotional dip from becoming a free fall was to ensure our customers got the best service they could get—defined by delivery in about 30 minutes.

Because we track and compare all of these numbers, sometimes our people feel pressured to fudge the numbers a bit, but I remind them that this information is a tool to help us serve the customer better, not a race in which something drastic is going to happen to whomever finishes last. I try to use only positive reinforcement to encourage my team to be accurate and honest with their performance indicators. We celebrate great performance, and we dig in to help when a team is faltering.

We also track food costs against an ideal number, which is based on cost versus sales. Like most other pizza places, we have a standard amount of cheese that goes on every pizza. Cheese is not only the most important ingredient on a pizza, it's also the most costly. As I write this, cheese is more expensive than it's ever been in my 25 years in the pizza business, accounting for 40 percent of the cost of a pizza. Maintaining a standard portion per pizza is vitally important: If we put on too much, we're hurting a store's bottom line; if we put on too little, we're hurting our customers. So we measure and measure and measure to make sure that we're providing the standard portion for our customers and that we're not falling victim to wasteful spending.

Our technology also allows us to track how many customers who are ordering by phone are put on hold. I don't use this information punitively, but as an educational opportunity. If I see that the majority of a store's customers are being put on hold between 5:45 P.M. and 7 P.M., for example, I'll point that out to the manager and ask what he or she thinks might be a good solution. The right answer is likely twofold: I would be looking for my manager to suggest scheduling an extra customer service representative to help with phone orders during that peak time and to suggest that we promote online ordering more aggressively.

➤ Make Your Objectives Real, and Make Them Known to Employees

When he began his professional career just after college, Domino's Pizza chairman and CEO David Brandon worked for Procter & Gamble. He learned many things from that prestigious organization, and one of them was the way it set goals and objectives.

From his days at P&G, Dave taught the company that objectives have to "SMAC," which is an acronym coined by P&G to note that every objective must be *specific, measurable, achievable,* and *compatible* to your company's mission. An example of a SMAC store growth objective for my company would be: "Open one net new store averaging $20,000 in weekly sales in Manhattan by the end of 2009." That would be specific, measurable, achievable, and compatible with my goal of continuing to grow my business. An example of something that would *not* be compatible with our goal of being the best pizza *delivery* company would be if I started drawing up plans for a 10,000-square-foot sit-down table-service restaurant called Domino's Pizza in downtown Manhattan. It's not gonna happen.

➤ Be a Resource for Your Team Members

As a coach whose job is to provide motivation, inspiration, education, and compensation, I have to be a resource for my team members, and that goes beyond just making sure I provide them with the essentials they need to manage my stores for me. Angie and I have helped identify some of our team members who would benefit from English as a Second Language classes, which not only helps them assimilate and feel more comfortable in the United States, but helps my business as well. My team members communicate more clearly, which benefits customers, and my employees are so grateful for the help that they become even more loyal than before. I also recommend many of the management books that have inspired me, such as *The One Minute Manager, Delivering Knock Your Socks Off Service, The Fred Factor, Psyched on Service, Common Sense Leadership,* and *Up the Organization.* My door is always open to provide advice or guidance, not only professionally, but I've also directed my team members to financial planners, recommended attorneys and accountants, and even helped them pick out a car!

➤ Give Your People a Reputation to Live Up To

Some years ago, the international division of Domino's Pizza honored me at the Worldwide Rally by presenting me with the "Ambassador of the Year" award, because I have hosted special Domino's Pizza guests from England, Australia, Japan, Turkey, Canada, Greece, Jamaica, St. Maarten, Puerto Rico, the Bahamas, and India (those are the ones that I can remember!). I remind my team that our guests visit all of us, not just me, because of our reputation for running great stores, providing exceptional service, and having a lot of fun. This would not be true without the team . . . and I reinforce the message that they have developed an incredible reputation for themselves and for my franchise—all they have to do now is live up to it! It is an honor and it is energizing to have peers from around the country and all over the world come visit you because of your reputation. My team members get it, and they are motivated to live up to that stellar reputation.

➤ Be Transparent, Not Intimidating

Sometimes owners are intimidating, but intimidation does not produce any kind of long-lasting positive effects. I've learned that if I make myself more "real" to my employees, I become less intimidating and they become more loyal. Here are a few examples:

➤ Every month, Angie and I conduct a meeting of our store managers at our office in Manhattan. Our office is actually a room dedicated to that purpose in an Upper East Side apartment; our meeting space is the living room. That means that every four weeks, my store managers come to a comfortable environment for a meeting of the minds. We provide soft drinks and snacks. We encourage them to make themselves at home. They sit on the couch or on chairs from the dining room. It's a cozy, warm meeting space, much better than a corporate conference room. Sure, they have to step over a sleeping dog (our border collie, Chief) and deal with the antics of a crazed kitten jumping on them while we're talking about the monthly profit and loss statements, but that just adds to the atmosphere of family communication, in my opinion.

➤ We keep the books open. Every manager in my franchise knows what his or her store's finances are; what fellow managers' finances are; how Angie and I make money and what the business costs us; and how much of the profits we're sharing with them. We are transparent in our business dealings. By taking the mystery out of it and sharing the details of the business openly, my store managers really do feel like owners, especially because they share in the profits.

➤ At our monthly meetings, we invite several store employees who are not managers or assistant managers. We do this for three reasons: We want them to feel welcome; we want to make the monthly meetings their bosses have to attend less mysterious; and we hope this will provide them with some inspiration to stick around and want to get promoted to management. They see at these meetings that we're providing information about bonuses and that we're constantly talking about ways to better serve our customers and take better care of our team members. At these meetings, they learn about new sales incentive ideas, and they see us award little things like Domino's shirts or other memorabilia we pick up when we visit the World Resource Center in Ann Arbor, Michigan. These hourly team members see that we try our best to respect the cultures our employees come from and to erase any barriers that might exist because of them.

➤ At our meetings, I let my managers open the proceedings. Taking turns, each one stands up to report the results of his or her store for the prior month. They talk about sales, service times, food, and labor cost percentages. They talk about results versus the goals they had set for each category. They talk about special things their team accomplished that month. They recognize a Most Valuable Person, who gets a $50 bonus and his or her name on a store plaque. They openly share what their goals are for the upcoming month. And they take this time to share what they need from us to make them successful, whether it's marketing materials, approval to create an in-store sales incentive program, or a new filter for the air conditioner. When they've had a particularly good month, they do a bit of good-natured trash-talking to their peers, challenging them to get better. It's all in fun and it serves to motivate them.

➤ When we teach classes to our managers-in-training, I like to invite hourly employees, too. The more people who know this stuff, the easier it is to make it a part of the culture of your operation.

➤ We take the time to get to know each of our team members personally, and to let them get to know us. I like watching the look of surprise on new employees' faces when I introduce myself, welcome them to our team, congratulate them on being hired by us, and thank them for letting us have 20, 30, or 40 hours a week of their lives! When you can come to understand and appreciate what's important to each individual, they will appreciate and respect what's important to you.

➤ Each summer we have a party for our employees, often at our home in rural Connecticut, which we've nicknamed "Camp Dave," because it is our retreat from the city. At these gatherings, we take walks through the woods, go canoeing, commune by the outdoor fireplace—but mostly, we just relax and enjoy each other's company. In 2008, we produced a calendar as a gift for all of our managers. The calendar is filled with photos we took throughout the previous year of fun events, activities, and trips we enjoyed. It is a collection of shared memories.

➤ We routinely take our managers on road trips to visit other successful franchisees. We've visited stores in New Jersey, Connecticut, and other parts of New York. We do this so that my team can meet other store managers, see

other operations, and share ideas for improving operations or local store marketing.

➤ I try to learn the basic or most-used words in the languages my employees speak. Even if you know only
a few words, being able to say "please," "thank you,"
and "good job" in their language makes them glow!
We have basic introduction-to-language books in our
library for several languages. Angie and I have purchased travel books about many of the countries our
team members are from to learn more about their
cultures. We've also "visited" their neighborhoods
using Google Earth to learn about the places where
our team members grew up.

➤ Accommodating different cultures is actually pretty
easy . . . and pretty interesting, too. We make it a
point to be flexible and to respect other cultures and
religions. Many of our team members are Muslim,
and an important observation of their faith is Ramadan, which is considered the most blessed month of
the Islamic year. During this month-long religious
observance, Muslims fast during daylight hours as an
act of deep personal worship, meant to teach them
self-discipline, sacrifice, and sympathy for those less
fortunate. At sundown, when they break the fast, they
often feast. Our team members will bring food to
break the fast to the stores, and at sundown, their fellow (non-Muslim) team members will happily cover
for them in the front of the store while our Muslim
team members go in the back to enjoy their evening
meal. Providing this opportunity and understanding
to them is extremely important—and, on occasion,
I've been invited to join them in this meal. It's a deli-
cious, authentic meal! I am honored to be invited, and
I find that they are honored to have me with them.

➤ Most important, you must let your team members know that you understand their need to be successful. In many cases, success is the ability to pay rent and feed their families. I also know that many of my team members save as much of their money as they can and send it back to their families in their homelands. That is no small responsibility. Angie and I respect that very much.

When they know you are there for them, they will be there for you, working harder than ever.

■ THE BEST PLACE TO START IS AT THE BEGINNING

So often in high-pressure, frontline industries like ours, it's common to see new employees leave within the first few weeks if they are not comfortable with the environment of the workplace. So it is crucial to connect with them on their first day and give them the training they need to be successful right from the start. I address this topic in more detail in Chapter 8, but I want to reinforce the importance of getting employees off on the right foot. My managers ensure that all new employees go through our New Team Member Orientation program before they put on a uniform and interact with customers. I make it a point to participate in these classes whenever I can. In addition to learning about our company, our philosophies, and our goals, we share with all new employees a list called "Expectations." This lets them know very clearly what we expect from them *and* what they can expect from us—this is another crucial step in ensuring a win-win relationship for both employee and employer.

Our Expectations of You

1. Arrive to work on time.
2. Have a great attitude—and *smile*!
3. Be in a clean, perfect-image uniform.
4. Hustle, hustle, hustle!
5. Work hard, keep busy.
6. Represent our company in a professional manner.
7. Ride your bicycle safely.
8. Go out of your way to delight the customer.
9. Do your part to keep the store clean and organized.
10. Use your best judgment.
11. You are authorized to make the customer happy.

What You Can Expect from Us

1. To be trained and challenged
2. A well-managed system
3. Great marketing and operations to keep business coming in
4. A safe and clean work environment
5. To be treated fairly
6. To be paid fairly
7. To have a fair and flexible schedule
8. The opportunity for growth and advancement
9. Open and honest communications with management

■ HAVE MORE FUN!

Now that I think about it, this is probably something I should have put closer to the front of the book, because this is certainly top-of-mind for me, for my team members, and for virtually everyone who works at Domino's Pizza. Heck, the company's motto is, *"Sell more pizza, have more fun!"* That motto comes at the end of our company cheer—yes, we really have one, and we do it a lot, especially when we're in public places like hotel ballrooms for manager rallies or other company events. It's a call-and-response cheer that goes like this:

Who are we?
Domino's Pizza!
What are we?
Number one!
What's our goal?
Sell more pizza, have more fun!
Sell more pizza, have more fun!
Sell more pizza, have more fun!

At our franchise convention in 2007, the Worldwide Rally at Disney World in Orlando, Florida, Domino's CEO Dave Brandon was telling the show producer during rehearsal about the cheer, and Dave mentioned he thought that when we were all assembled, we could be louder than a jet plane. The producer was skeptical, to say the least, and bet Dave $20 that the audience could not beat the decibel level of a jet airliner during our meeting the next day. Dave took the bet. The following morning, during our opening general session, Dave told the audience about the bet. He pulled out a decibel meter and put it at the front of the stage, in front of a television camera projecting the meter onto four massive screens facing the audience so we could all see our progress. Dave mentioned that, according to some quick Internet research, a jet airliner on takeoff hits 110 decibels. Then he started the cheer. By the time we hit "number one!" our 3,500 voices had hit 112 decibels and the producer was already running down the aisle to hand Dave his twenty bucks onstage.

We make sure we celebrate every success we can. If a store sets a weekly sales record, Angie and I will be there with a cake to share with the team to acknowledge their hard work. (No matter where they're from, we've discovered that people really enjoy cake!) We never let an event go by without making sure we photograph it, because people also love to see pictures of themselves having fun.

Another thing we love to do is host store visits, particularly with first-grade classes. Kids at that age are old enough to understand what we're doing, and they have so much fun! Our team members do, too—they love to show off their stores. During these visits, we divide the kids into teams: "Pepperoni" and "Cheese." The Pepperoni team comes out to the front of the store, where they wash their hands, then get to play with the dough, see the computers, and put pepperoni on some pizzas. The Cheese team goes in the back and into the walk-in cooler; they get to wobble a bag of pizza sauce and fold a couple boxes. Then we see which team can scream their team's name the loudest! Carryout customers and people walking by the store love it. My friend Ben Asen's son Ivan toured our store when he was six years old. In 2008, he graduated from the University of Miami, and he still remembers his Domino's Pizza store tour: He's been a loyal Domino's customer ever since.

AMERICAN DREAM EMPLOYEE: EMIR LOPEZ

Out of the Projects, He Returned to Give Back to His Community

When Emir Lopez was ready to open his first Domino's Pizza store, he could have done it anywhere. But after working his way out of the James Weldon Johnson Project in East Harlem, New York, Emir decided the best place to open that store was right in the neighborhood he had come from.

Born in Puerto Rico, Emir came to New York when he was four, brought over by his mother. He was raised in the Weldon Project, a cluster of ten 14-story buildings in the heart of East Harlem, known by most as Spanish Harlem. During his youth, Emir focused on education as the way to get out and make a better life for himself.

"I wanted to be financially independent," Emir says. "I wanted to enjoy life, and I knew I had to work hard to get there." The path he took, however, was not the one he expected.

Emir worked his way through the New York Institute of Technology and graduated with a degree in architecture. He landed a job after graduation and was on his way . . . until he was laid off, which often happens in tough economic times. Disillusioned, Emir gave up architecture and went in search of something else.

"I thought I would go into the food business, because I really love food—I love to eat," he says. "I wanted to get into restaurants with the idea of owning my own one day." He applied to a few culinary schools, but they weren't offering scholarships. Still paying for his architecture degree, he decided not to take on more debt for additional schooling. By happenstance, he saw an ad for a manager-in-training position at Domino's Pizza.

"I applied for the job and went to interview with Jim Denburg," he recalls. "I wore a suit and tie that day. It was the middle of July and it was *hot*. Everyone else waiting for an interview was in T-shirts. I guess I made an impression, because Jim took me to meet Dave Melton."

Hired as a manager-in-training, Emir plunged himself into the job, often working up to 80 hours in a week. "People at first thought I was crazy to take a job making $4.15 an hour, especially because I was in debt from college. But I decided to bite the bullet and pay my dues. Within six months, I was a general manager."

Emir managed Dave's 89th Street and Third Avenue shop for more than three years before deciding he was ready to open his own store. Domino's Pizza was expanding rapidly at the time, and opportunities existed throughout the United States and across the globe. Emir's choice for his first store: East Harlem, where no other delivery business had ventured to this point.

"I could have franchised anywhere. I even considered applying to be the master franchisee for Brazil," he says. "But I grew up in East Harlem. I'm just a kid from the projects. I did what I had to do. I went to college, got myself started, and came back to my old neighborhood to open my own business."

He opened his store on a Friday in April 1996. During his first three days in business over that weekend, sales topped

(Continued)

(Continued)

$18,000. The first full week he was in business netted $27,000 in pizza sales. Knowing that East Harlem presented even more opportunity, he opened a second store soon after. "I've been a franchisee for 12 years, and I love being in my store. I love hiring and recruiting. I love the flow of the business. I want to raise sales, serve my customers, and make money for the long run," he says.

Emir has given back to his community in many ways, not the least of which was being a pioneer in providing hot food delivery to a community that felt shunned. "Nobody would deliver to the projects. Nobody," he says. "Then along came Domino's, and now everyone wants to deliver here. Do I feel like a pioneer? Absolutely. A lot of my competitors saw that I was delivering here and they've gotten into delivery, too. I'm okay with that. Competition makes you work harder."

Emir donates pizza to people who volunteer to maintain and repair the gardens in the projects, and he also donates pizza to organizations dedicated to children. He sponsored an event in which he fed an entire school. During the annual East Harlem Puerto Rican Festival, which draws half a million people to the neighborhood during the weekend, Emir gives out pizza slices and branded items to anyone who passes by.

For a businessman who had the opportunity to leave the projects behind but didn't, does Emir have any regrets? "There have been moments that have been rough," he admits. "Safety and security can be a challenge. Winter is tough, because we deliver on bicycles. Delivery guys are not thrilled about going out on bikes when it's negative 10 degrees outside. My brother helps out in the winter. He's a got a car . . . which I bought for him. But no, I've never regretted it.

"I love Domino's Pizza. I love that I had the opportunity to own my own business. I love that I can give back to my old neighborhood. I still have the passion for this business that I had when I started."

Chapter

5

Next, Teach Customer Service

"We guarantee our service and our product. Our team wants you to be completely delighted. If you have any comments, please call our Customer Care line at 212–426–1734."

That number, printed on all our advertising flyers, rings straight into my home office. Several great things have happened as a result of publishing it. First, I began to get important feedback from my customers that they may have felt uncomfortable sharing with the store directly. More important, my team knows that a customer can get in touch with me directly, and they know that I follow up on every call I receive and fulfill every customer promise I make. That directly affects team member behavior at the stores.

I also specifically chose the word *delighted* instead of *satisfied* because I think that just meeting a customer's expectations isn't enough anymore. You need to make them say, *"Wow!"* People will talk about an experience that left them delighted; if they were merely satisfied with what you had to offer, that's nothing to brag about. You can delight a customer by exceeding their expectations . . . by delivering more than you promise, especially if they've come to you with a complaint. In our franchise, if a customer doesn't like his or her pizza for whatever reason, we'll apologize without being defensive, make a fresh one, and deliver it to that customer—and give the person something extra for the inconvenience.

So, why have a chapter on customer service in a book about hiring and retaining entry-level employees and turning them into long-term, valuable contributors?

> ➤ If you're reading this book, you are likely a business owner or manager, or perhaps you are someone who aspires to be one someday. The entry-level frontline employees you hire are the face of your business—they are the people who have the most direct interaction with your customers. Therefore, they have the most impact on whether those customers come back.
> ➤ Your company exists to serve and delight customers. The more you can do that, the more your company will grow and succeed. Customers, especially repeat customers, are the key to your growth.
> ➤ Your frontline employees need to know that their success, growth opportunities, and rewards are directly related to their ability to delight customers. In my franchise, as in most of Domino's, that connection is easy to make. The manager of a successful store makes more money through a share of the profits. Delivery team members earn more money through tips when the store is busy than when it's not. In-store team members are rewarded with bonus opportunities when sales increase. At a more basic level, people's livelihoods depend on our ability to delight customers. There is a lot of competition out there; thousands upon thousands of food establishments

and restaurants are competing for the same customers, and customers vote with their wallets. If we fail, we close—and everybody loses, especially my team members who would be forced to find other means of employment.

➤ People want to be part of something special, and these days a company that truly values its customers and its employees is special. A company that meets the needs of customers and employees will have great sales, and that translates into more income for employees and more profit for the business owner.

That's why there's a chapter on customer service in a book like this. Let's proceed.

■ MAKE IT PERSONAL

One of the things I preach to my team when it comes to product and service is to "make it personal." By that I mean two things: First, no matter how many pizzas we sell, individual customers are only concerned about the one *they* ordered, so we have to make that pizza specifically for them. Let them know that we made the pizza personally for them by the care and quality we put into it. Second, when it comes to service, "make it personal" means addressing them by name, smiling and being friendly, and making sure we take care of their concerns by putting *their* needs ahead of ours. "Make it personal" means making and delivering pizzas with such care that each customer thinks we are in business solely to please them. If you are a manager of frontline team members in a retail business, isn't that how you'd want all of your customers to feel?

One of the things I try to instill in my team members is perfecting the "three-minute performance." That is, one minute on the phone with the customer and two minutes at his or her door. Those three minutes are the most customers actually interact with team members from the store. We have to make those few minutes count; we need to use them to make our customers say *"Wow!"* I equate it to being on stage in a Disney production or at one of Disney's theme parks. At Disney, employees are "cast members" and customers are "guests." Disney teaches its cast members that when they're onstage—that is, when they are interacting or even remotely visible to guests—they are truly "on." Disney sells a magical experience. We're trying to do something similar, but in a radically condensed time frame!

Here are some of the things you can put on your own "make it personal" checklist:

➤ Smile!
➤ Be polite and friendly—you are always "on" while at work.
➤ Let customers know you are happy to see them or to have them call us.
➤ Ask customers how you can help delight them today.
➤ Listen to their needs and do your absolute best to fulfill them.
➤ If a customer has a concern, listen to it completely, without interrupting.
➤ Ask the customer how they'd like us to resolve the concern and to best meets their needs, and do your best to accomplish that.
➤ Apologize when it's needed.
➤ Remember, the customer is always right!

I take the "make it personal" approach to managing and accommodating the special needs of my team members. If I can meet their needs and they can meet mine, we both win.

Remember, when I hire, I'm looking for warm people, not warm bodies. I look for people who:

➤ Aspire to succeed
➤ Want to learn
➤ Care about our customers
➤ Care about their coworkers
➤ Don't lower their standards or expect me to lower mine
➤ Have a passion for what they do
➤ Are not afraid of hard work
➤ See the opportunities that lie before them—and are inspired by them

■ THE CUSTOMER IS ALWAYS RIGHT—NO, REALLY

Stores, and entire businesses, have personalities. They reflect the values and attitudes of the owner and the people in charge. You already know that Domino's Pizza emphasizes *Fast and Nice* in virtually every store around the world, and that our internal motto is *Sell more pizza, have more fun!*

I want my stores to be happy, positive, and have customer-oriented operations. Whenever I interact with a customer, whether I'm taking a pizza order or handling a concern, I make sure I'm living up to and demonstrating not only the behaviors I want from my team, but my very values as well. I also make sure I demonstrate those values *after* my interaction with a customer. While it might be tempting for someone to mutter "what an idiot" about a complaining customer behind his or her back, what does that teach your team? That you don't really believe the customer was right? That you're just faking it?

If I directly handle a customer complaint in the store, I will talk to my team after the interaction and ask them if they understood what just happened, what the customer's concern was, and how I handled the situation. I also ask them how I could have handled it better. By soliciting their input and having them come up with solutions, they learn faster and take ownership of handling future issues. These are the best opportunities to teach—with real-life examples. This is also how my team developed their own procedures for handling customer complaints, called "Turning *Ow* into *Wow*," which is included in the last chapter of the book.

A customer who is calling our store back with a complaint is really just a loyal customer giving us a second chance. I am so *grateful*! I find that if I resolve customers' concerns in their favor right away, they will be more loyal than customers who have never had a problem. These customers now know that we really do stand by our promises, and if they ever have an issue, it's okay to call us and it *will* be fixed. The alternative is a customer who doesn't call back . . . ever. That's not an alternative I'm willing to accept.

Many years ago, my friend Phil Bressler raved about Stew Leonard's grocery store in Connecticut. The thing Phil loved most was the sign posted on a huge rock outside the grocery store for everyone to see:

Rule #1: The customer is always right.
Rule #2: If the customer is ever wrong, re-read rule #1.

That is the attitude you must instill in your team members, and the best way to do that is to live it yourself and demonstrate it every chance you get.

I tell my managers: "Don't run this store to make *me* happy. Run it to make the customer happy. I buy very few pizzas here, and it's the real pizza buyer you need to delight." It's the customers' money that's in our bank accounts; if they leave, so does their money. It's a pretty simple equation.

Domino's franchisee Gene Lancaster, who owns stores in Indiana, was featured in his local newspaper in 2008. In it, he talked about his perspective on customer service:

> My . . . mentor, Richard Mueller . . . taught me that if you focus on customers, the bottom line will always take care of itself. (It may cost a bit more, but) just make the customer happy. In my experience, the average happy customer tells three friends about his or her experience; the average disappointed customer tells six or more. So, to net more positive word-of-mouth, you need to invest heavily in your reputation and taking care of people.

■ SERVICE, SERVICE, SERVICE

Marketing to attract new customers is expensive; working to keep your existing customers coming back costs less. All you have to do is make them feel the difference between *satisfied* and *delighted*.

For us, this means making great pizzas, delivering them fast, and being friendly. When customers call or order online, it doesn't matter to them how busy we are, nor should it. It doesn't matter that my manager may have 30 pizzas to make, because that particular customer cares about only one.

That was another thing Phil Bressler talked about a lot when he was a leader at Domino's Pizza. Customers always have to believe they're first in line and that it doesn't matter how busy we are. Customers order only one or two pizzas at a time, and they eat pizza only one slice at a time, one bite at a time. We have to show meticulous attention to detail and do it over and over again.

Here in Manhattan, we marvel at the talent and incredible performances to be found in the theaters on Broadway.

I used to wonder how those actors could perform the same material night after night, until I realized that they *don't*. While the core of what they do is the same, every night is different, because every audience is different. The actors might be marking their hundredth performance, but most members of the audience are seeing them for the first time. The actors have to bring fresh energy to the play every single time. That's the same in almost every service or restaurant business: Customers eat meals one at a time—they don't care how busy you are or whether you are tired or think you created your masterpiece for the couple at table 6. They want their meal to be perfect, too.

During my new employee orientation classes, I let everyone know that they are authorized to make the customer happy on the spot. They can do whatever it takes to turn a customer with a complaint or concern into someone who is surprised and delighted by the response. I also let them know that if they ever feel like they "got in trouble" for making that decision, they can let me know, just to reinforce that everyone on my team is authorized (and expected!) to make customers happy. My home number and cell phone are posted on the schedule board at each store. I tell everyone that my door is always open and anyone is welcome to call me at any time. My team members know they can share my phone numbers with anyone who asks for them.

■ LOOK AT YOUR BUSINESS FROM THE CUSTOMER'S POINT OF VIEW

There is likely not a single retail business in the country that couldn't improve if the owner or people in charge occasionally viewed it from the customer's perspective instead of their own.

Drive up one day in the middle of business hours and see what your customers see:

➤ Is the storefront inviting?
➤ Is the parking lot clean?
➤ Do the windows sparkle?
➤ When you walk in, is the shop brightly lit?
➤ Are the walls bright or dingy?
➤ What kind of energy does the store give off?
➤ Do the team members seem happy to be there?
➤ Do they greet you with a smile?
➤ Are they happy to see you?
➤ Are they busy or bored?
➤ Can customers find what they need without confusion?

Look at the product your business is serving:

➤ Would you buy it?
➤ Are you proud to serve your product to a paying customer?
➤ Would you serve it to someone you were trying to impress?
➤ Would you serve it to your mom?

At our monthly manager meetings, we call our own stores to hear what our customer service representatives sound like. As you read in a previous chapter, what we want and expect to hear—in less than two rings—is the voice of a person who's smiling (yes, you can hear smiles over the phone) saying, "Thanks for choosing Domino's Pizza. My name is Dave. How may I help you today?" A fellow franchisee, Charlie Malament, who owns stores in Maryland, insists that every customer hears this: "Thank you for calling Domino's Pizza, *where we love our customers . . ."* That almost never fails to take a customer by surprise, especially someone calling for the first time.

What we don't want to hear is a rushed, distracted voice that says a sentence so fast it sounds like one word: "Domino'spleasehold." We use these occasions to determine whether there's a training issue or a scheduling problem at the store. It's usually both, and they present opportunities for improvement.

We also call our competitors and order their products to see how they answer the phone, how easy the ordering process is, how the customer service representative treats us, and how "fast and nice" their service is—or isn't. When I plan to make these calls in advance, I tell my managers to come to the meeting hungry. Time seems to go slowly when you're waiting for the doorbell to ring. It goes even more slowly when you're hungry. This activity helps our team members empathize with the hungry, waiting Domino's Pizza customer.

If I walk into a store and I see a pizza that isn't a great one for whatever reason (not enough toppings, too many bubbles in the dough, overbaked crust), I'll point it out to the crew, then I will toss it out.

I want my team to see that impressing a customer is more important than food cost. I set each store's food cost goal at a small percentage above "ideal" food cost in the budget, which leaves enough room for the store to discard pizzas that aren't up to our standards. Of course, my team realizes that it's more important to make pizzas right the first time. If you don't have time to make it right the first time, when are you going to have time to do it over? Besides, remaking a pizza adds another seven minutes to the customer's delivery time, so it's even more crucial to make pizzas right the first time.

Before the oven tender (the quality control person ensuring all orders are prepped for delivery) closes the box, I want him or her to take a good look at that pizza and imagine what the customers will say when they open the box at home. If that pizza doesn't make you say "wow!" when we close the box, there's no way it's going to change on the trip to the customer's door!

My friend Don Meij, who calls himself the Chief *Enthusiasm* Officer of the Domino's master franchise company based in Australia and who you'll read about later in this book, shared with me the Seven Absolute Rules for Customer Service that they follow Down Under. With his permission, here they are:

1. Never tell a customer that a problem or product can't be fixed! If a customer is not satisfied, you *must* do something.
2. Don't worry about whether the solution will cost too much. As you serve customers more effectively, there will be fewer expensive problems.
3. Never promise too much, and always do a little more than you promise to do. You build credibility by doing more.
4. Treat your customer's needs first. The organization's need is to maintain customers.
5. Give all customers a fair deal. Don't give special service to one and try to "make it up" on another.
6. Fix the problem right the first time you handle it.
7. Accept the fact that sometimes a customer will take advantage of you.

I want to reemphasize Don's last point. This is where many businesses get into trouble. For reasons I can't quite understand, many businesses refuse to accept that *maybe* they made a mistake, got an order wrong, or messed up a customer's order. They ignore "the customer is always right" rule, and behave as if a customer with an issue or complaint is somehow trying to cheat them.

Perhaps, just perhaps, 1 percent of the people who call with a concern are doing so because they're trying to get something for nothing. So what? You can't treat the other 99 percent of your complaints that way. Accept that fact, but more important, accept the fact that sometimes you do screw something up, and it's your job to fix it.

Another way I look at my business from the customer's point of view is to ask my customer service reps which offers customers ask for the most. Based on their recommendations, we have tailored offers to meet customer demand. One of my top customer reps, Robert Lugo, suggested an add-on coupon for wings and a soft drink for $7.99 with the purchase of large pizza, because he saw a trend of people ordering pizza, wings, and Coke who were always looking for a "deal" with that order. At the store, it's now called the Robert Coupon, and he's very proud of the recognition.

■ COMPLAINTS ARE OPPORTUNITIES

I've seen that message in virtually every book on service I've ever read and heard it in every speech I've attended. Do you know why? Because it's true: The way you respond to an issue or concern often has a greater impact on your reputation, and on your customer's future purchase decisions, than the issue itself.

As you're reading this, your mind is probably taking a subconscious inventory of recent customer interactions you've had in which you have been the customer. Maybe it was at the grocery store, your local bank branch, an airline counter, a gas station, or a restaurant. If you had okay experiences, you are likely hard-pressed to remember them. But if you were insulted or just treated as a number, it's probably more top-of-mind for you, and I'm bringing up a bad memory. (Sorry!) But if you had a concern and the business *wowed* you in response, that's probably even more top-of-mind, because it's so rare these days.

Here is one of my favorite recent *wow* stories.

A friend of mine and his wife stayed for two nights at the Timbercliffe bed-and-breakfast in Camden, Maine, in July 2008. After the first night, one of the proprietors, Karen, asked whether the couple was enjoying their stay. My friend's wife, who has some issues with her back, mentioned that she had a bit of difficulty sleeping because the mattress in the room was too soft.

Immediately, the proprietor apologized and personally took them into each of the three available rooms in the inn and let my friend's wife try out each bed to see whether there was a mattress firm enough for her. She found one that would work, and the owner insisted the couple move into that room for the next night, even though that room was bigger and more expensive than the one they had originally booked.

Now, that was responsive customer service, but it didn't end there. My friend was expecting to pay the original agreed-upon amount for the two nights they stayed at the Timbercliffe, even though the second night was in a deluxe room. But the inn owner surprised them even more at checkout by insisting my friend would not be charged at all for the night his wife had trouble sleeping!

They ended up in a more spacious, more expensive room for a lower rate and got one of two nights free—even though this issue was not the fault of the B&B. The owner told my friend and his wife, "This is not about us; this is about you. We want you to be happy." That is *wow* customer service!

Another story on a different note involved my friend Phil Bressler. One day while he was at his store, a customer came in to pick up a pepperoni pizza, but he had only a hundred-dollar bill in his pocket. Phil's customer service rep at the front of the store was struggling to figure out what to do. The order was legitimate and the customer was offering payment, but the company policy was not to accept bills larger than a twenty. Many retail shops have policies like that for safety reasons and because they need to have enough change available for other customers.

When Phil learned about the issue at the front of the store, he sprung into action. He took the pizza and handed it to the startled customer. Phil told him, "I'm sorry we can't accept bills larger than a twenty, so tonight's pizza is on us. Sorry for the inconvenience. We hope you enjoy your dinner."

Phil's crew was flabbergasted until he explained to them that the customer very likely made an honest mistake and wasn't trying to pull a fast one. The cost of the pizza was minimal compared to the impact giving it to him would be in return business. Instead of insisting the customer go get change for his hundred-dollar bill before he could get his pizza, the customer had been *wowed* by Phil's response. "How many people do you think he's going to tell that story to?" Phil asked. For a brief moment, some of Phil's crew thought that other people might come in with big bills and try to do the same thing, but then quickly realized how silly that sounded. Nobody ever tried it . . . but that original customer came back again and again, and always with the correct change. For the cost of a $10 order, Phil got the value of hundreds of dollars of marketing—and sales!

Whether it's a family-owned bed-and-breakfast in Maine or a pizza shop in Manhattan, *customers want you to solve their problem, not create another one.* My team knows that it usually takes a lot for a customer to call back with a complaint. It's much easier to accept a mediocre product with so-so service and just go somewhere else next time. Of course, many people these days won't do that without telling their friends about their bad service when they go to work the next day, and in these days of blogs, e-mail chains, and social networking sites, one person with an issue can complain about you to thousands of others.

Opportunities to deliver good service and bad service make themselves available all the time. The bad ones are often surprising, because you realize that they could have turned out differently with just a little bit of effort.

A friend told me about the time he went for a passport at his local post office branch on a Saturday. He was in line at 1:20 P.M. He watched as a customer in front of him had his passport processed. When my friend got to the counter, it was 1:32 P.M. He was asked if he had an appointment. No, he said, he didn't know he needed one. There was no indication anywhere in the office that appointments were needed on Saturdays. He was told that the post office processes passports only until 1:30 P.M. on Saturdays, unless you have an appointment. My friend said that his paperwork was complete, his photos were ready, and besides, he had been in line at 1:20, and it was only 1:32, and all he needed was someone to stamp his paperwork. Couldn't they just do it and not make him come back again? "The clerk punches out at 1:30," he was told, and he had to make an appointment and return another day to get his paperwork processed.

That's the kind of hourly mentality you want to avoid as a business owner, even if you have hourly employees. If post office branches were run like retail franchise businesses, chances are the service levels would improve. By the way, my friend reported that when he did go back for his appointment, the entire process took only six minutes. The passport processor would have been able to provide some meaningful customer service and still punch out at 1:38, instead of making my friend return to the post office another time.

■ YOU CAN NEVER "WIN" AN ARGUMENT WITH A CUSTOMER

Yet so many people get defensive and actually end up arguing about who is right in a customer dispute. As I've mentioned, it's expensive to drive new customers to your business to try your product or service. It's easier and less expensive to take care of an existing customer and make him or her happy.

If a customer with a problem is giving you the chance to fix it, then fix it! That person will be more loyal to you than the customer who didn't let you know about an issue—and will be even more loyal to you than the customer who never had a problem in the first place.

But let's say you *do* argue with a customer. Even if the customer is wrong and you "win" the argument, what comes next? The customer leaves and never does business with you again.

Did you really win?

Chapter 6

Create a Common Language of Incentives

In May 2008, each of our four stores had a record sales month (that was exciting!), so Angie and I gave $1,000 to each manager to distribute to their teams in any way they saw fit. We had only two requirements: (1) The managers could not keep any of the $1,000 (because they already share in the store's profits), and (2) every employee in the store should get *something*. Handing $10, $20, or $50 to a team member who went above and beyond in the course of his or her job does incredible things for morale—and keeps employees coming back for more! They want to set more records, because they know they'll share in the success. Such is the power of incentives.

Generally speaking, people like to compete. They like to test themselves and be challenged. Most important, people like to win. Being rewarded for it? That's icing on the cake. It doesn't matter where they're from, what language they speak, or what job they do—people like to succeed and be acknowledged for it. Because I consider myself a coach, and I believe in positive energy and positive reinforcement, I believe that incentives are the single greatest tool I have for motivating my workforce . . . and they can be for you, too.

Incentives work—whether the person receiving them is the manager of a retail business, an executive at a large corporation, or an entry-level employee making minimum wage. And incentives don't have to be pure cash, although I have yet to find a team member who would ever turn it down. I'm going to get into some of these ideas in more detail, but incentives can be almost anything:

- ➤ Pins or badges for uniforms to acknowledge certain accomplishments
- ➤ Shirts or jackets that indicate that the wearer achieved a specific milestone
- ➤ Certificates of achievement, plaques, trophies
- ➤ Dessert (yes, you read that correctly!)
- ➤ Parties
- ➤ Tickets to movies, concerts, or sporting events
- ➤ Gift certificates to a popular restaurant for the employee and a guest
- ➤ Electronic gadgets like MP3 players or tricked-out cell phones
- ➤ Gift cards
- ➤ Watches, rings, or other kinds of jewelry
- ➤ High-definition televisions
- ➤ Trips
- ➤ The list is limited only by your imagination!

Parents use incentives all the time, whether it's the promise to purchase a coveted toy if Johnny will stop sucking his thumb or the offer to buy the "big girl bed" once Emily doesn't need to wear diapers anymore. Parents offer incentives for good grades or positive behavior in school. We learn at an early age that rewards for achievements can be quite addicting—we like to get that "something extra" when we achieve success in challenges that lie before us. Incentives work not only with individuals, but with entire groups of people—like the kids in the elementary school who pledged to read 1,000 books during the school year instead of watching television after school. The payoff: If they reached their goal, the principal would call an assembly and have a barber shave off all his hair in front of the entire school. That's a fun and creative way to reach schoolkids, and it's essentially free . . . that principal was really using his head!

And that's one of the true beauties of incentives: Many of them don't actually have to cost anything, or not very much, anyway. As an employer, you can offer anything, from a paid day off to tickets to a movie for your employee and a guest. You can offer to sponsor a pizza party for your team if they hit a sales milestone. Angie and I like to acknowledge certain achievements with a cake for the crew—people love dessert, especially when the boss is paying!

When I started working at Domino's Pizza, my supervisor, Frank Meeks, loved to come by the store and offer incentives for the crew. Sometimes he would put a 10-dollar bill on the counter in front of the customer service representatives and tell them that the money would go to whomever sold the most cans of Coca-Cola-with-pizza orders in the next 60 minutes. Or he would offer $10 to any of the pizza makers who could make a large pepperoni pizza in less than 60 seconds.

Frank went on to become one of the largest and most successful franchisees in the history of Domino's Pizza, and his love of incentives grew as his company did. He had a standing offer to his employees: He would buy an individual the car of his or her choice if any of them ever won the annual Domino's Pizza World's Fastest Pizza Maker competition (which has its own incentives, like a free trip to Las Vegas and a cash prize of $5,000). In the first 15 years of the competition, an employee of Frank's "Team Washington" won the competition *nine* times! It became so commonplace for a Frank Meeks team member to take home the trophy, the company named the trophy after him when he passed away in 2002.

As I progressed through the ranks while working for Frank, he promised me an incentive I was happy to go after. Frank wrote me a handwritten note on a small piece of paper that said, "Dave—When you quit smoking, I'll make you vice president of Domino's Pizza of Washington, D.C., Inc." Talk about a real win-win opportunity for me! I did quit smoking, and Frank lived up to his promise. I think Frank was inspired to offer that kind of incentive by Domino's founder Tom Monaghan, who once offered a major cash bonus to a vice president of his who was overweight. Tom was concerned about the employee's health and well-being and in the early 1980s offered him $50,000 if the employee could complete a full 26.2-mile marathon within one year. The executive did it, and Tom happily wrote the check.

Like Frank Meeks, I love to offer small cash incentives to challenge my pizza makers or encourage my customer service reps to promote sales of a side item or a new product. When we introduced Oven Baked Sandwiches in late 2008, our 32nd and Third Avenue store manager, Jewel Mannaf, was challenged by four other stores to sell the most sandwiches the first week. Each store put in $100, and at the end of the week Jewel's team had sold over 550 sandwiches and all shared in the $500! When I do that, the store crews are not only enticed by the idea of the cash incentive, but by the good-natured bragging rights that come with finishing on top. (One of the things I've learned since working with so many immigrant team members is that trash-talking is universal!) I will also routinely pick out shirts and other items with the Domino's logo and present them to managers or team members who finish first in a challenge I present them, like lowering the number of customer concerns, reducing bike thefts, or improving their "out the door" times. The company also has a special line of pins that pizza makers can earn for their uniforms, based on how fast they can make a large pepperoni pizza.

■ INCENTIVES CAN WORK FOR ANYONE

Domino's chairman Dave Brandon loves to offer incentives, too, even to franchisees. One would normally think that a business owner would have enough incentive just to see his or her business succeed, and, as a business owner, one of my top priorities is to provide incentives for *my* own team. However, I am still motivated by the incentives offered by Dave Brandon and the parent company. Every year, the top 2 percent of Domino's franchisees are awarded the International Franchise Association "Gold Franny" (a trophy that looks a bit like the Oscar trophy for motion pictures)—the single highest honor presented at the Worldwide Rally. While Angie and I have a shelf full of those trophies on display in the living room of our Upper East Side apartment, believe me, we can always make room for one more! It has been extremely gratifying to receive that trophy in front of my peers from around the world, for they know best how hard it is to run their own franchises and what it takes to be considered among the best.

Years ago, company founder Tom Monaghan added his own twist to the prestige of the Gold Franny. He not only presented the top franchisees with the trophy, but Tom gave us all gold sports jackets, which he wanted us to wear at all future award programs. They looked a little strange, actually, but those of us who were fortunate enough to get those jackets wore them proudly.

Dave Brandon upped the ante in 2008, when the company had a monthlong sales challenge, and the top 100 franchisees were invited to a cruise to the Bahamas with the Domino's executive leadership council. Dave also invited all of that year's annual award recipients to join the sales challenge winners for the awards celebration that took place at the Atlantis resort in Nassau.

In 2001, Dave created the "Chairman's Circle Hall of Fame." Almost every year, Dave selects a franchisee to be inducted into this very exclusive "club." In addition to a plaque with their portraits etched in crystal on permanent display in the welcome center of the company's headquarters in Ann Arbor, Michigan, Dave presents each inductee with a Presidential Rolex watch, inscribed with their name and featuring the Domino's logo on its face.

It's important to share stories of how your top performers achieved their goals with your entry-level team members. These stories of achievement and reward can inspire your newer team members to become top performers themselves. In the meantime, it's also important to have incentives for your minimum-wage and entry-level team members, because you want them to "catch the fever." Many of my franchisee peers in other parts of the country award $25 and $50 gas cards as incentives to their delivery drivers who excel at customer service. These days, I think a gas card would be enticing to anyone who owns a car! No matter what business you're in, you can create incentives around things you want to accomplish. Perhaps your goal is to improve the safety record of your team and reduce accidents and injuries at your warehouse or on your construction site—if so, create and offer an incentive to that end.

RPM Pizza, the largest Domino's franchise in the United States, offers a full 40 hours of pay as a cash bonus or a full week of paid vacation to every one of its delivery team members who reach 2,000 hours of safe driving, defined as no at-fault accidents or tickets for moving violations. If your goal is to reduce customer complaints, then offer incentives when your team improves service and reduces complaints by 10 percent, for example. If you want to speed up production of a product, offer incentives to motivate your team to increase production by a certain percent while maintaining or improving quality.

For my hourly employees, specifically my delivery team members, three incentives are built into the job from day one: *tips,* the *work schedule,* and *assigned job duties.* Obviously, for a person whose job is to deliver hot food to hungry customers, a big motivation is the opportunity to earn a tip from the customer who has been delighted by the service you provide. My team members know that a friendly, smiling face is better than a frowning, unfriendly one. Customers love to know that you hustled to get their pizza to them, so my team members often note the delivery time when greeting the customer: "Here is your hot Domino's pizza, delivered in just 18 minutes!" It also pays for a delivery person to hustle back to the store because the quicker they can get back for another order, the more customers they can deliver to, thus increasing their chances for more tips. And, as I mentioned in an earlier chapter, my delivery team knows that part of the job is to help us sell pizza, not just to deliver it—that's an incentive opportunity they can control.

We've got posters hanging in our stores that feature CEO Dave Brandon's "Tips for Tips," which provide four proven techniques that help increase the likelihood of being rewarded by customers. These were originally targeted at pizza delivery team members, but I've edited them slightly so that they are applicable to anyone whose compensation includes tipped wages.

Tips for Tips

Make eye contact. As the door opens, look the customer in the eye and say, "Hi, how are you today?" Customers are used to delivery people being relatively quiet. Be different. Set yourself apart.

Smile! It's the single biggest thing you can do to help yourself. People do not want to tip a delivery person (or waitperson) who doesn't look happy to see them.

Say thank you. As you hand customers their order, tell them, "Thanks for ordering from us tonight. We appreciate your business." This will increase your chances of getting a bigger tip.

Wow the customer's concern. Sometimes things don't go as planned. The customer could be concerned (but not necessarily complaining) about the time of the delivery or about the product itself. If you find yourself in a situation where the customer shows concern, follow these three easy steps:

➤ *Apologize.* Make a personal apology. Say, "I am sorry that we are running later than expected tonight," or "I am sorry that you are unhappy with your order."

➤ *Give the customer what he or she wants.* Take care of customers' needs on the spot. If they are not pleased with the order, offer to call the store and have a new order sent out right away. Let them keep the first order . . . never ask for it back.

➤ *Give them something extra.* Customers who show concern remember people who went out of their way to give a little something extra. Add a free beverage or side item to the order and apologize again for the inconvenience. They will remember you took care of them and will probably tip you even better next time.

■ ANYTHING CAN BE AN INCENTIVE— EVEN THE WORK SCHEDULE

Hustle pays off. And that's where the work schedule and assigned job duties come in as incentives. In our business, we want our best delivery team members to work at the busiest times . . . and virtually all of our employees *want* to work during those peak times, because the busier we are, the more money they can make. I have no problem, for example, getting people to work for me on New Year's Eve or Super Bowl Sunday—those are great days to earn tips. My managers know that scheduling people to work at peak times can be a motivator. If you're a delivery person, your opportunity to make money is at the customer's door, not in the back of the store folding boxes or mopping the employee restroom or while you're off duty. In my stores, you have to earn your way into being scheduled during peak times, and you have to earn your way into the opportunity to deliver.

My managers use the schedule to motivate people to achieve by letting their best people set their own schedules and select the best jobs around the stores. The middle performers get to pick the shifts that are left over. Those team members who are chronically late or don't demonstrate the kind of hustle we want are assigned a schedule and get assigned jobs like cleaning the grease trap and the restroom. These employees can use this as an incentive to improve—and many of them do—or they leave.

If you manage a business that features tipped wages for your employees, you can use the schedule to reward your best, most efficient, and friendliest employees, too. Schedule them when the opportunity to earn the most money exists, such as a Friday night or whenever your peak business hours are. Instead of using the slow times to punish your weaker employees, entice them with the opportunity to get a better schedule with better performance.

■ SET GOALS, DEFINE SUCCESS, AND LET YOUR TEAM KNOW HOW TO WIN

For an incentive to work effectively, you have to give your team a target to shoot for. It is one thing to say that you will reward the team if sales go up or if the number of returned items goes down, but that would be too vague. Does one more sale versus last period equal *up*? Do three less returns versus last month equal *down*? You must make sure that your goals SMAC (i.e., that they are *specific, measurable, achievable*, and *compatible*) so that your team is in the best position to tackle the challenge. Start with the end in mind. Let's say that your target is a reduction in lost workdays due to accidents or injuries on your job site. Set the goal for your team by giving them a SMAC objective: *Our objective is to improve productivity by reducing the number of lost workdays by 10 percent during the next three months versus the previous three months.*

An objective like that is specific, measurable, achievable, and compatible with your goal of increasing productivity, reducing costs, and having a safer workplace. You can announce an incentive if the objective is reached, such as a $50 bonus to every member of the team, an evening outing to a local sports event, or some other noncash token that will be appreciated by your employees and that they're willing to work for. Another popular and easy incentive is to have a raffle at the winning store for a nice prize like an MP3 player. For some employees, the incentive might be an evening of bowling together. Once you set your target, you can work backward to develop the ways in which your team can reach it. Those ways could include daily reminders of the goal by the supervisor, a chart counting up the number of accident- or injury-free days, or a training refresher course on best practices for safety on the worksite.

Keeping score is an important way to know how you're doing when your team is trying to reach a goal. If your team doesn't know how they're doing, they can lose the motivation to keep working toward the goal. It would be like playing baseball without keeping score . . . not nearly as much fun. If you ever visited one of my stores, you would see a lot of posters showing our sales in the current week compared to the previous week and the previous year. You would see the load time of pizzas, the time out the door, our week-to-date and month-to-date sales, and many other key indicators of how we're doing. What gets measured gets done!

Summer is a sales killer in New York City. Some people think it's too hot to eat pizza (I emphatically disagree!), and on the weekends, everyone with the means to do so gets out of the city. We had some choices: We could either accept it or do something about it. We chose the latter and created the Summer Sales Challenge, which runs roughly from Memorial Day to Labor Day. All of our store teams compete against each other to see who can achieve the highest percent sales increase versus last year during that time period. The winning store gets new shoes for each team member, gift certificates from the company's Equipment & Supply Division for shirts with the Domino's logo, and cold, hard cash. We update the teams each week so they know where they stand. During the past five years, this has helped our crews focus on *building* sales through promotion, offering lunchtime deals to local businesses, or whatever creative way they can think of, instead of just lamenting that business is slow. Although summer sales are still not as strong as they are during cooler months, we've seen more growth than we had previously.

In a retail environment, you can create an incentive around overall store sales improvements, a line of products, or even a single product. About once each year, Domino's Pizza and Coca-Cola will team up for a "Say It and Win" promotion designed to encourage customer service representatives in all Domino's stores to promote add-on sales of Coke to pizza orders. "Mystery shoppers" will call stores throughout the country and order pizza; if the person taking the order asks the customer if he or she would like to add an ice-cold Coke with the order, the customer service rep automatically wins $50.

Stores that increase incremental sales of Coke products the most during the promotion win prizes for their entire teams. In your retail store, you can team up with one of your vendors for a similar incentive program that will drive sales of the vendor's product and increase revenue for you. Incentive programs that benefit employees, business owners, and suppliers are another example of win-win-win thinking.

■ KEEP YOUR PROMISES

Once you set the goal, define success, set up the challenge, and determine the reward, it's time to let your team go for it on their own, knowing that you are supporting them and that you will *keep your promise*. Nothing crushes morale or weakens an organization more than a leader who promises a reward but then doesn't deliver. Use your SMAC objective and your incentive to motivate your team, and they will work hard for you. Break a promise, and it will take a long time to get their trust back—if you ever can.

I know of a manager of a movie theater who routinely hires high school kids at minimum wage to sell tickets, work concessions, and clean up the theaters between shows. He promises fun work and the opportunity for raises. The problem: Once he gives one of his employees a raise (even if it's a dime or a quarter an hour), he almost immediately cuts their hours or keeps them off the schedule entirely, so they're not making any more money than they did before they got the increase.

The result is that many of them quit in frustration, disillusioned because they thought they had done the job well enough to get a raise, but are being penalized for it at the same time. As for the cinema manager, instead of keeping motivated employees for a few years during their high school careers, he keeps them only a few months, and he's constantly interviewing, hiring, and training new minimum-wage employees. He's being shortsighted by watching the pennies on the payroll and missing the big picture of the many benefits he'd gain by having a well-trained, reliable team that will come to work and make the movie-going experience a more enjoyable one for his customers. How much more productive could he be if he wasn't constantly interviewing and training new employees? He's losing out simply because he won't deliver on his promises.

■ SURPRISE YOUR TEAM WITH DEGREES OF REWARDS

Some managers who use incentives often go about it in a strictly black-and-white fashion. For example, if the goal is to increase sales for the period by 15 percent and the team falls short, there is no payoff. That's okay . . . sort of. If you set a goal and fall short, it does make sense *logically* to withhold the incentive, but does it makes sense *emotionally*? Probably not, especially if your team was close to achieving the goal. I know some people who embrace the idea of surprising their employees with varying degrees of rewards. Here's what I mean: If you set a sales improvement goal of 10 percent, and your team falls short but increases sales by 8 percent, why not reward them somehow? Who's disappointed with a sales increase of any kind these days? If they did their best and worked to achieve the goal, reward them for that. It does not have to be the full payoff of the reward, but they're going to appreciate some kind of acknowledgment for their efforts and for their success.

Imagine your team giving its best and falling just shy of their goal. Their initial reaction is going to be disappointment—until you come in, thank them for their effort, and surprise them with a degree of the incentive. If the pledge was a $50 bonus if they raised sales by 10 percent, but they raised sales by only 8 percent, surprise them by saying that everyone gets a $25 bonus. At least they got something for a good effort. Imagine what a morale booster that would be! They would know, tangibly, that you appreciated their extra effort, and they will reward you with loyalty and continued effort.

Likewise, consider increasing the reward if your team exceeds its goal. Let's say you promise a cash bonus for achieving a sales target. If your team meets the target dead-on, you pay them 100 percent of the bonus amount. If your team *exceeds* the target by 10 percent, surprise them by giving them 110 percent of the promised bonus. Better yet, tell them up front that 110 percent success equals 110 percent reward, 115 percent success equals 115 percent reward, and so on. That is the kind of *wow* for your employees that will come back to you with energy, excitement, and effort every time.

■ SHARE THE SUCCESS TO MAKE PEOPLE THINK—AND ACT—LIKE THE OWNER

Management books everywhere encourage executives to get their people to think and behave like owners. That is sound, important advice, but unless someone truly *feels* like an owner, it's difficult for them to think or act like one. This is why, from the very beginning of Domino's Pizza, it has been common practice to reward managers with a share of their store's profits. Nothing makes you feel more like an owner than sharing in the business's success. It worked for me back in Quantico, Virginia, and it works for my managers in Manhattan, just as it works for thousands of Domino's managers the world over.

Any retail business can benefit from giving its managers something to work toward besides an annual salary. Profit sharing or performance bonuses change the way people think and behave. If managers know they're going to share in the *bottom-line* success of the business, they won't just focus on driving top-line sales—which are extremely important— they'll also pay attention to managing the costs associated with operating the business. Your managers will also focus on scheduling to ensure they have just the right number of employees on hand during your peak times so that every customer is served; they'll work on employee relations and retention so that they're not constantly recruiting, hiring, and training new people, which is a costly endeavor. They'll focus on building repeat business with customers, because it's less expensive to bring an existing customer back than it is to market for new ones.

Minimum-wage employees benefit from this kind of thinking in two ways: Great managers who are treated like owners provide incentives to their hourly employees to drive performance; and entry-level employees who know that management opportunities come with profit-sharing programs are enticed to advance their careers with you, thus creating more loyalty among your top performers. It's worked for Domino's for almost 50 years, and it's worked for me: Every one of my store managers started as an entry-level hourly employee; now they run million-dollar businesses in which they share in the profits. That's great for them and great for me. It can also be great for you.

AMERICAN DREAM EMPLOYEE: SHAIK SHAMIN

The American Dream Remained Strong Even After September 11
In 1996, when he was 19, Shaik Shamin said good-bye to his parents in Bangladesh and came alone to the United States. Like others before and since, he was looking to fulfill a dream that could only be found in America. A year later, he thought he had found it: as a bartender in New York City.

He enjoyed his job, especially the money, and was quite content until a friend of his told him about his job delivering pizzas for Domino's. "My friend said it was huge fun,"

(Continued)

(Continued)

Shamin recalls. "I could make $200 in tips on a Friday night at the bar, but having fun is more important to me, so I came to work here."

He started out, as most do, delivering pizzas on bicycle. "Biking is very tough," he says. "Six or seven hours of continuous biking—that's very hard, but I loved the energy and meeting a lot of people."

In his first week on the job, Shamin worked from open to close because he wanted to immerse himself in the job and learn as much as he could. He loved making customers smile and getting to know them. He is naturally upbeat and genuinely nice—perfect for a bartender or a pizza store manager who would eventually go on to become Domino's first-ever Fast and Nice Manager of the Year.

Shamin became one of the top delivery guys at the pizza store on 32nd Street, and he was thriving, until the night his bike hit a patch of ice and he slid under a car at an intersection. He broke his shoulder and was out for three weeks. "It hurt, but worse, I hated being away," he says. "I loved the job."

The time off to recuperate gave Shamin time to think about his future. He decided that his future belonged in management and, eventually, business ownership. He came back to the store and jumped at the chance to become an assistant manager. In 2000, he got his chance to lead the 32nd Street store in Manhattan.

Shamin brought his passion for fun to the job of general manager. "I try to make everything a game," he says. "I like giving my team challenges. My goal is to make every employee happy. We're all responsible for achieving the goals—we can't do that without teamwork. And we always remember that the customer is the boss."

If Shamin sees a customer who hasn't ordered from him in a while walking past the store, he'll go outside and start a conversation. "I'll say I'm sad that I haven't seen them in awhile and I'll offer them something free if they come back and order from me. Nobody else does that. I want my customers to know that I recognize them and I appreciate their business."

Shamin also believes in leading his team by example. He refuses to give orders; instead, he asks team members if they would do him the favor of mopping the floor, or folding boxes, or cleaning the restroom. He won't hesitate to do those jobs himself to make the point that no job is beneath him.

Even though he is the store's chief pizza maker and manager, he asks his delivery team members to be responsible for quality control. Shamin's delivery team members open every pizza box to determine whether the product is good enough for them to deliver. If it's not, they won't hesitate to ask Shamin to make a new one. "Most delivery guys don't care if the pizza is bad—they're just delivering a box and handing it over. My guys won't let us deliver a bad product. I like that. That means they care."

In the eight years Shamin managed the 32nd Street store, his team broke every sales record that existed, from hourly to annual sales. He is now managing the flagship Manhattan store on 89th Street as he prepares to own his own franchise.

"Domino's Pizza gives us the key," he says. "But we make it all happen."

Shamin probably doesn't realize it, but he made it happen in the days following the tragic events of September 11, 2001. Shamin learned of the devastation the way most of us did: on television. When he watched the tragedy unfold, he knew he had to get to his store, which was the one nearest the World Trade Center.

"People were getting out, and I was getting in," Shamin recalls. "I knew we had to open because everything else was closed. People were going to need food."

He drove as far as he could: to 125th Street, then walked 93 blocks to the 32nd Street store. When he got to the store, he called every employee he knew who lived in or near Manhattan and asked them to come in. "They all had to walk, because the buses and the trains weren't running. When we opened, I was the only one available to make pizzas. We tried to deliver on the first day, but had to stop because there were just too many people coming into the store. We could only handle carryout business and donations," he says.

The next day, when the police realized Domino's was open, some officers came in and asked for pizzas they could take to the site of Ground Zero. From there, the floodgates opened. Shamin worked 18 days nonstop, often up to 14 hours a day. The store stayed opened around the clock to meet the

(Continued)

(Continued)

demand. For three days, Shamin slept when he could in the back of the store.

"We had some employees come in but not enough," Shamin recalls. "Nobody could get in to the city for those first days. The police kept coming in for more and more donations, so I taught some officers how to make pizzas. It was something to see officers in uniform on the makeline or at the cut table. Customers in the store were so touched and energized when they saw New York cops making pizza for the rescue workers. It was incredible."

Shamin remembers a call he received early on from Domino's chairman and CEO David Brandon. "Mr. Brandon called me and asked me what we needed. He told me to just keep making pizzas, because the company was going to be paying for all the food. We ended up giving away a thousand pizzas a day right after the attacks."

Shamin was honored by the NYPD and the Highway Patrol for his efforts, and he's justifiably proud of what he and his team did, but he's also humbled by the accomplishment. "We had to open," he says again. "People needed food. We were the best ones to get it to them."

Chapter 7

Teach the Benefits of Honesty, Hard Work, Loyalty, Teamwork, and Trust

One of our guiding principles is "We demand integrity." That is a simple, powerful message to send to new hires and veteran employees alike about the way they are expected to behave whenever confronted with a difficult choice. It lets people know that the company expects integrity from team members, executives, franchisees—even its suppliers—and that they can expect the same in return. Integrity and trust are the foundation of any relationship, personal or business.

Honesty and integrity are crucial links between supervisor and employee because that relationship determines how your employees interact with your customers. At my franchise, my team members and I talk about honesty a lot, because it's very important to me and I want it to be important to them. We talk less about the consequences of poor choices and more about the benefits of good ones. My team knows, because I've demonstrated it, that I won't stand for breaches in integrity. For example, here's an obvious one: You cannot steal from me—period. I consider being rude to a customer the same as stealing, because when an angry customer leaves my business, so does his or her money! Being rude to a customer is a job-ending act in my stores. Equating rudeness to stealing is a surprising concept to people the first time they hear it, but once it sinks in, they go out of their way to ensure they don't drive away a customer ever again.

President Harry S. Truman famously had a plaque on his desk that said, "The buck stops here." That was his way of saying he accepted the responsibility of making the tough decisions and would be accountable for the results of those decisions. I believe the same principle applies to honesty and integrity—it starts with me, the owner. If I want it, I must first demonstrate it. The manager of the cinema I wrote about in the Chapter 6, who gives young people raises and then cuts their hours so they don't really make more money, models entirely the wrong behavior to very impressionable minds.

A friend of mine in the public relations industry provides counsel to executives and business owners. He puts the message this way: "If you want to be perceived as something, *be* that something." If you want people to think of you as community-minded, get involved and do good things. If you want to be trusted, be trustworthy. If you want people to think of you as honest and ethical, the answer is clear. Employees will model the behavior of their employer, particularly their immediate supervisor, which is why it's very important to hire good managers. Businesses, whether they're pizza shops, office environments, or construction sites, take on the personality of the leader. If the leader doesn't model good behavior, neither will his or her team. I model the behavior I desire and expect from my team—especially to my managers. They are the ones closest to me, and, likewise, they are closest to their crews.

In his autobiography, Domino's founder Tom Monaghan says, "Honesty and ethical behavior *can* be taught. Managers can sometimes do it by example, and it's an uplifting experience for both manager and employee when it happens. But if a person lacks integrity, attempting to work a character change is tough."

■ SITUATIONAL OR BEHAVIORAL INTERVIEW QUESTIONS CAN GIVE YOU INSIGHT INTO AN APPLICANT

Traditional questions are too easy. Rather than just asking standard questions like, "How long did you work at X Company," or "What would you say is your greatest strength?" managers can ask situational or behavioral questions in job interviews. Here are some examples:

➤ Tell me about a time when you dealt with an angry customer. What was the issue, and what did you do to resolve it? What was the final outcome?

➤ Tell me about a time when you were asked by a supervisor to do something you were not comfortable with, such as lying to a customer. How did you handle it?

➤ Tell me about a time when you were asked to cut corners or compromise on quality. What did you do?

➤ You see your manager "skim the till" and put cash into his pocket. What would you do? Knowing that you saw him, the manager offers you half the cash. What would you do?

➤ You witness a colleague, who happens to be a friend, mistreat a customer, behavior that you know is an absolute "don't." How do you handle it? What do you say to her? What do you tell your supervisor?

Questions like this challenge people because they draw on their personal experiences and force them to deconstruct and explain previous actions, which are strong indicators of future behavior. Sometimes you'll find that people realize that they made a poor choice and learned from it. Sometimes you'll discover they didn't think skimming from the till was all that bad! Even if you ask a situational question and applicants don't have an actual experience to draw on, ask them how they think they would behave in that situation. That also gives you insight into how people think.

The head of security at Domino's, George Ralph, has been involved in law enforcement for nearly 40 years. George says that, on average, if given the opportunity to steal from you and get away with it, 15 percent of your workforce will do so without hesitation, 15 percent will never consider it and the remaining 70 percent will have to think twice before they make their decision. George's advice is to do your best to remove the *opportunity* for people to steal from you. Why test the 70 percent when you don't have to? My advice is to hire well, model the behavior you expect, act swiftly when there is an issue, and constantly reinforce the benefits of making good choices. In my franchise, when we succeed, everyone shares in the bounty. Those who would steal from the store are not just stealing from *me*, they're stealing from themselves, their colleagues, and their friends. When we discuss the challenge of making difficult ethical decisions at my manager meetings, I often ask my team members to consider what it would be like if they had to explain their actions to their family, or if what they did were to be reported in the Sunday newspaper. If they cringe at the idea, they realize the answer lies in another direction.

Jewel Mannaf, who has worked for me since 1995 after arriving in the United States from Bangladesh, told an interviewer once that the thing he appreciates most about working for Angie and me is that we "are all about hard work, honesty, and loyalty. They [Angie and I] teach you how to work, how to behave honestly. I won't ever leave because of the respect I get here." Coming from a valued team member, that is high praise indeed. Modeling the behavior we want is easy for Angie and me, not just because we're inherently honest, but because the rewards of our positive behavior have enriched our lives—quite literally.

■ WORKING HARD AND LOVING IT

I've never been afraid of hard work—in fact, I relish it. In the beginning it was not uncommon for me to work 70 or 80 hours a week to get my stores up and running. My stores could get as many as 150 orders in a single hour during peak times. The frantic pace, the close quarters, the heat of the massive pizza oven, and the constant movement of a dozen employees is an energizing, exhausting kind of work. For those first few years as a franchise owner, I barely made any money. In fact, I paid no personal income tax, because I didn't earn enough to qualify. During our first full year with a store in Manhattan, Angie made a nice salary working in a bank, but our joint tax return showed our net income was *negative* $17,000! But I refused to give up on my dream. Eventually it paid off well.

The American Dream often requires sacrifice, belief in yourself, and yes, hard work. This is behavior I modeled and still do. The rewards eventually came, and my managers now benefit from them, too. I tell this story to my team and back it up with the incentives to prove it.

➤ Manage by Example

In your workplace, the best way to motivate your team to work hard (and work smart) is to model it. Do you have to be the first one in and the last one to leave? Not always, but you should be occasionally. After all, who has more of a vested interest in the success of your enterprise than you? If you run a clothing store, for example, why not vacuum the floor or get the clothes from the dressing rooms and put them back on the racks? If you run a restaurant, why not pitch in and wait on customers or wash dishes in the back? If you supervise a team of hourly workers doing manual labor, why not work beside them during a shift on a regular basis?

Breaking a sweat with your team says a lot more about you than any words could. I still jump in to make pizzas during a rush or breakdown and restock the pizza makeline when it needs to be done. My team members have also seen me make a large pizza in 50 seconds, mop the floor on occasion, and rotate the inventory in the walk-in cooler. There was a trend in the 1990s called "management by walking around" (thanks to a great book by management guru Tom Peters). That's great advice, but I prefer "managing by *example*." Proving to your team that you're willing to do any job you ask of them, rewarding them for their hard work and achievement, and demonstrating your commitment to honesty and integrity can go a long way toward building loyalty.

TRAINING REDUCES TURNOVER

In the quick-service restaurant industry, turnover rates are as high as 100 percent or more a year, which means that every hourly worker employed in a given restaurant on January 1st will leave and be replaced at least once before the year is out. That turnover rate is almost as high in many other industries, especially among hourly employees. Many new hires leave office environments within the first three to six months; in the retail sector, new employees leave within the first two weeks (some people have been known to quit after the first shift!). The primary reason for such quick turnover is that new employees don't feel properly welcomed—and by that I mean that they are thrown into the fire without any kind of sufficient preparation or training. Supervisors often say that training personnel properly is too time-consuming, especially because they're always looking for new people. They may not realize that if they did a better job at training up front, new employees wouldn't feel overwhelmed and would stick around longer.

Human resources professionals will consistently tell you that the first weeks of a new job are the most crucial. Some would say it's the first day. Try this little experiment right now: Think back on what your experience was on your 952nd day on the job. You can't—because so many days are alike. You're comfortable and you know exactly how to do your job. Now, think about your *first* day on your current job, or the first day of your first job. Chances are, the memories came flooding back, because that first day is so pivotal—it leaves a lasting impression. You can create a welcoming experience by taking the time on your team members' first days to greet them, introduce them to their coworkers, and provide them with the base training they'll need to feel comfortable. The first day is a big step toward building loyalty.

◼ LOYALTY CAN BE EARNED BY CREATING A SENSE OF TEAM

Loyalty can be earned, and to have a great team, it must be. Your team members don't have to just be loyal to you, the manager or owner. They should be taught that loyalty to their fellow team members and to the company itself is important. There is power, strength, support, and camaraderie in a tight, loyal team. Your team members want to be successful. Your job as a manager or owner is to help make them successful, because that's the way your enterprise will grow and prosper. Rewarding team members for their achievements is one way to do that.

When I opened my first store, I did the bulk of the on-the-job training. I quickly realized, though, that if I wanted to open more units, I would have to hire and train managers, who would in turn hire and train my employees. Making my managers part of my team was essential. Some of the ways I do this are as follows:

➤ By sharing profits
➤ By providing them with educational opportunities or giving them the time to pursue their own studies
➤ By providing resources to do the job and trusting them to make good decisions

Today my managers lead a team-oriented training approach—beginning with having a peer be part of the initial interview process. From there, the veteran members of the crew pitch in to train new hires. The veterans reinforce for the new employees the standards we expect, the fundamental tasks of the job, and they foster the culture of the individual store—a culture built around exceptional customer service and rewards for all.

That support from fellow employees means a great deal to entry-level team members, especially if they are working their first job or are new to the country, which is often the case with my employees. My employees understand this: *They are valued members of the team, but no one is bigger than the team.* They win as a team; they lose as a team. Individual contributions are important, of course, but when challenged, we will always make decisions in the best interests of the whole group. For me, it works, as evidenced by the fact that the average tenure of my employees is eight years—in an industry where I "should have" replaced each one of them more than 12 times in that time period.

All of this ultimately boils down to trust. From business owner to hourly employee to manager, we all trust each other. I trust everyone on my team to pitch in, work hard, and take care of our customers. My team members trust me to take care of them, provide them the support and resources they need, and offer the incentives that motivate them.

➤ Dealing with Problem Employees

That culture of trust is evident when an employee isn't getting the job done quite right. Rather than jumping to any negative conclusions, my managers and I work with the team member to find out whether he or she doesn't know how to do the job or just doesn't want to. We let the problem employees tell us. If they don't know *how*, we'll help retrain them and support them in the learning process. If they don't *want* to do the job, we'll take another course of action. Either way, we show respect and support. The culture of trust and loyalty also made itself known during the situation I wrote about in Chapter 2, when my team asked me to fire a colleague whom they witnessed pocketing cash from carryout orders. The team didn't want a thief in their midst.

➤ Create a Pledge Form for Your Employees to Sign

We set the tone of our expectations with a pledge form that all of my employees sign before beginning their jobs. It is a simple, nine-point document called, "I Promise." After new hires have successfully completed my New Team Member Orientation class (which I often teach, because it's that important to me and I love teaching it), they read and sign the "I Promise" pledge. The pledge reinforces the essential elements of their role, and because they are signing their names to it, they are making a commitment and a statement about their personal character. For my immigrant employees, character is vital, and signing the "I Promise" pledge is not something they do lightly—so when they sign it, they *mean* it. You can come up with your own pledge to meet the needs of your business, but here are some ideas:

> ➤ I promise to arrive on time and ready to work for every shift I am scheduled to work.
> ➤ I promise to put safety first in my job.
> ➤ I promise to do my best to delight every customer.
> ➤ I promise to treat people the way I want to be treated.
> ➤ I promise to do the best job I can on every project I am assigned.

Here is the "I Promise" pledge from my store on 89th Street. You'll see that it covers everything from how employees will conduct themselves to what day of the week the oven gets cleaned.

I Promise . . .

> ➤ To make sure the order is complete and dispatched every time.
> ➤ To call out the time in the oven, call the time out the door, and call the delivery time on every single pizza.
> ➤ To treat the customer with courtesy and respect in every situation.
> ➤ To help the store increase sales by participating in promoting.
> ➤ To commit myself to increasing my knowledge of my job through training.
> ➤ To provide our customers with a *wow* experience every time.
> ➤ To clean the office thoroughly every Monday, clean the oven every Sunday, clean the walls and doors every Thursday.

➤ To observe all safety policies and conduct myself to avoid accidents.

➤ To help make 89th Street store the best Domino's Pizza store in Manhattan.

■ INVOLVEMENT IN THE COMMUNITY BUILDS TEAM SPIRIT

Another ingredient I've found crucial in developing loyalty and team spirit is community involvement. Doing good things for people and organizations in your community is important: It makes you feel good; it's good for business; and it boosts morale among your employees. People like working for organizations they can be proud of. Many minimum-wage and entry-level workers can appreciate what it's like to be in need, and knowing that you devote time, energy, and resources to helping those less fortunate can mean a lot to them. In my stores, we have been involved with count-less charities, including the Leukemia/Lymphoma Society, St. Jude Children's Research Hospital, Ronald McDonald House, the Pediatric Cancer Foundation, Asphalt Green, and dozens of churches, schools, and other charities.

My managers are encouraged to seek out and support charitable organizations that are special to them in some way. As a franchise, we donate thousands of pizzas each year to not-for-profit groups, schools, and other organizations that are having volunteer meetings or fund-raisers. We've fed blood donors, people walking for a cure, and, as I noted earlier, police officers, firefighters, and rescue personnel in times of tragedy.

If your business has a favored charity, encourage your team members to volunteer, and give them paid work time to do it. Invite them to join you on a team for a fund-raising walk on a Saturday, or offer to match donations if they go out and solicit funds on behalf of the organization. You can invite employees to nominate charities, and then you can conduct an election to determine which will be your "charity of choice" for a year. The possibilities are endless, and so are the rewards of giving back to your community and letting your employees play a part.

In the end, I absolutely believe that you *can* teach honesty, hard work, trust, and teamwork primarily when you reinforce the benefits to be had by them. You will gain loyalty when you succeed at doing so. Finding people of solid character is essential, and the first place to look for one is in the mirror. Everything you get from your employees is a reflection on you. What do you see when you take a close look?

Chapter

8

Connect on a Personal Level: Show Respect, Appreciation, and Support

I love helping people develop, gain experience, and succeed. For example, I've watched people come through our doors scared of their own shadow and practically unable to speak to another employee. Several months later they are buzzing around handling everything like the experts they've become. I've helped five of my managers go on to become franchisees themselves, and they own nearly 20 stores between them.

This is something I'm extremely proud of, one of the aspects of my job that gives me the most satisfaction, and it is part of the fabric of the Domino's culture—franchisees helping their managers become franchisees themselves— that's how the company has grown. People like Frank Meeks and Dave Wood, two very successful franchisees I worked for, helped me get my start. I knew that I owed it to them to help others, just as they helped me.

Of course, this was not really what I was thinking about at the beginning when I was trying to build my own business during those first challenging months. Although I had opened and operated stores in and around Virginia (including in Washington, D.C., which was no cakewalk), I was not fully prepared for the size, the energy, and the diversity that is New York City. In Virginia, when I managed my first store, I was accustomed to hiring marines stationed at Quantico who were working a second job—people who were, from a cultural perspective at least, much like me. New York City is vastly different.

In 2000, the foreign-born population in New York was 2.87 million, or 36 percent of the city's 8 million people. At that time, more than 43 percent of the city's foreign-born population was made up of recent entrants, meaning they had come to the United States within the previous decade. Nearly half of them had come from Asia and 44 percent from Latin America. New York City truly is a melting pot of cultural diversity.

What did that mean for me? The short answer: a lot of learning about other cultures, as quickly as possible. I knew that the majority of my future employees would be foreign-born or born into families of recent immigrants. One of my first visits was to Asi Sheikh, who supervised a collection of stores in Brooklyn that were owned by the Domino's corporation. Born in Pakistan and raised in the United States from the age of 11, Asi, a graduate of the University of North Carolina–Greensboro, is now executive vice president in charge of Domino's Pizza Inc.'s 500-plus company-owned stores in the United States. (Asi's story is featured later in this book.)

Asi's team at the then 30 stores in Brooklyn was made up almost entirely of foreign-born team members from many different countries. I asked him what he thought I needed to do to connect with my employees and be successful. His answer seemed simple enough because the message truly resonates no matter where you're from. The message is universal.

■ RESPECT THEM, AND EARN THEIR TRUST

"Trust and respect are the most important things," Asi said. "In many developing countries, men are treated like kings at home, and they expect that kind of respect on the job. They can easily leave and find a job somewhere else, so if you want them to stay and be productive for you, the first thing you need to do is show them respect. Don't yell at them, especially in front of others. They will tune you out very quickly."

The first piece of that idea neither surprised nor concerned me. I've never been one to think there is ever anything to be gained by yelling at, intimidating, or humiliating someone. I have always believed in positive reinforcement, coaching, and positive energy.

"The other thing is that they have got to trust you," Asi said. "And only you can make them do that. They've got to know that you're not out to exploit them or take advantage of them. Once they trust you, they'll break their back for you." Respect and trust have always been tenets of my business, so Asi's perspective reinforced my beliefs and helped take away some of my anxiety about working with people from other countries and cultures. What I've learned since then is that while people are different, we are also similar; while our backgrounds might be light-years apart, our goals, dreams, and aspirations are often quite alike. Ultimately, we all want to succeed in whatever endeavor we choose; we all want to be able to provide for our families. Respect and trust go a long way in every relationship.

Your entry-level and minimum-wage employees are likely getting their first work experience with you, and it's up to you to show them these things so they can start off on the right foot. As I've said, if you value your employees so that they can really feel it, and if you provide them with the resources to succeed, you won't have to worry about how they're treating your customers.

■ MAKE IT PERSONAL: LET YOUR EMPLOYEES KNOW THEIR WORK IS IMPORTANT AND APPRECIATED

My team members are often new to the workforce and are getting their first real on-the-job experience. They are also often new to the country, so they are challenged by a new culture, by a new language, and occasionally by prejudices that exist. They can be anxious about being in a new place, meeting and working with colleagues from different cultures, ethnicities, and political and religious backgrounds. They can be intimidated by the idea of working with customers face-to-face. They can also be intimidated by the business owner. That is one of the first things you should address with your new employees: They shouldn't be frightened of you.

Whenever I visit one of my stores, I make it a point to seek out anyone who has just joined our franchise. You should see the look on their faces when I introduce myself, welcome them to Domino's Pizza, and thank them for giving 30 to 40 hours of their life to us every week. I tell them that I appreciate that commitment and pledge to be a resource for them. It's a great feeling to see their reaction. I also take the time to ask them what they're here for—what they hope to accomplish. Obviously, the first answer is that they want to make money and to get some valuable work experience. I let them know that this is definitely a place where they can make money: All they have to do is listen to their manager, learn as much as they can about the business, and work hard to delight our customers—from there, anything is possible!

I have seen some workplaces where the employees dread the visits from the owner, who either seldom visits or, when he or she does, just comes in to inspect and criticize, not motivate and inspire. If your entry-level employees flinch when you walk in the door, you definitely have some work to do. People join your company because they want to earn money and experience—that's a given, but you must also remember that people want to *succeed*, even in hourly work. Your job is to help them!

Consider the point I made in the previous paragraphs: Your employees are dedicating 30 to 40 hours a week of their lives to work for you. This is an intriguing paradigm shift; they're not just putting in hours for minimum wage, they're giving you valuable hours of their lives. In the high-turnover environments of entry-level, minimum-wage, frontline work, you know your employees can always go somewhere else, because they often do! You will definitely treat them differently when you realize that today's solid employee can be gone tomorrow.

Take the time to connect with your team members. Get to know them personally. Make sure they realize that you understand that they are human beings, valuable in their own right, and not just spokes in a wheel or interchangeable parts of some mechanical device. Your employees have family . . . parents and siblings, spouses and children. Some of them are working their way through college; some of them may not have finished high school. They have dreams and aspirations; they have worries and fears. They have senses of humor. Let them know the same things about you. "Make it personal." People not only enjoy working for someone they like and admire, they want to work harder when they're working for someone they truly like.

Share with your employees the importance of the role they play in your business. Whether they are part of a team manufacturing a product, washing cars, taking tickets at a cinema, or serving customers in a more direct fashion, if you have hired them to fill a need for your business, it must be a necessary role. Therefore, the person filling the role is crucial to your success. I make it a point to give every employee my home and cell phone numbers, and they know they are welcome to call me anytime they have a question or are facing difficulty.

■ PROVIDE FLEXIBILITY

Listen to your employees' concerns, dreams, and aspirations. Share with your team members the opportunities that exist for them when they work hard and help your business grow. Those opportunities could be anything from incentives and bonuses to advancement to higher levels in your organization. One of the least expensive incentives or benefits you can provide your team members is flexibility. I prefer to think of myself as a realist, and that means I know "stuff happens." People don't live a nine-to-five existence anymore, so if you have a business that can accommodate flexible schedules, offer them.

One of the attractions to employees of Domino's Pizza is the flexible hours in the stores. While Domino's Pizza is the only job for the majority of *my* team members, delivering pizzas is a second job for 60 to 70 percent of the employees at Domino's stores nationwide. Many people use pizza delivery for supplemental income and enjoy working in the evenings in an energetic, customer-friendly environment. It pays to be flexible if your employee base is made up of students, who not only want to earn money, but they need time to study and manage the hectic schedules that come with academic life. In my stores, I let my better performers select and set their own schedules. At first blush, you might think that this would be a problem, because I need people—and my best people—on Friday and Saturday nights, times when most people would rather be anywhere but work. However, my best employees know that the busiest times are not only the most challenging and fun, those are when they make the most money . . . so letting them pick their own schedules is another win-win-win situation. My customers get the excellent service of my best team members, who are making good money and driving sales for me.

The other element of flexibility to consider relates to your employees' cultural and religious backgrounds. Religious rites and ceremonies are important, and you can build loyalty among your employees when you show that you understand and respect their beliefs. I've already mentioned the accommodations we make for our Muslim employees during the month-long observance of Ramadan. To be honest, it's not much of an accommodation, because their fellow team members are more than happy to handle the store's business while their Muslim coworkers break their daylight fast with a meal in the evenings.

Flexibility for religious rites is easier when you have a diverse team. One of the common mistakes hiring managers make is hiring people like themselves . . . meaning, they overlook the benefits of hiring people of different races, cultures, ethnicities, and religious backgrounds. Not only will you benefit from different perspectives and ideas, but another benefit of having a diverse team is that if you run a retail operation, you don't have to close for the holidays!

What do I mean? Because most of my employees are Muslim or Jewish, December 25 is not a holiday for them, for example, nor is it to many of my customers. Although most stores throughout most of the United States are closed, the Domino's Pizza stores in New York City are open on Christmas Day. In fact, it's one of the busiest days of the year because so many of my competitors are closed. We also benefit from an extra day of sales because we are open 365 days a year.

■ HELP THEM LEARN

Anyone coming to work for you is there to earn money, of course. But many of them want to learn and grow. Helping them will go a long way toward turning entry-level team members into long-term employees. I don't just mean helping them learn the basics of their job, although that is important. I'm talking about teaching them about business in general. Employees will be more engaged and involved when they understand how their role impacts your organization. Teach them how your business makes money, what expenses you incur that affect profitability, and how they can help generate revenue or lower costs. I teach my employees about the importance of customer service and what great customer service looks like. I teach them how their store's profit and loss statement works and how their actions impact that. Training is a constant in all of my stores.

Angie and I will also help our team members when they need some additional educational assistance. We have helped employees improve their English skills by supporting them in their English as a Second Language classes. We help employees who are new to the country ensure that they are registered and maintain their legal status and all of their paperwork. It is not uncommon, I've learned, for many immigrants to come to the United States to establish themselves before they bring their families over to live with them. Many of my employees send money to their families back in their home countries while at the same time they're accumulating savings to bring over wives and children. Asi Sheikh's father, for example, worked in the United States as a college professor for seven years before he brought his wife and two sons to live with him.

Angie and I have loaned money to some of our team members to bring their families over sooner than they otherwise would have been able to afford because we realize how important it is to keep families together today. The team members we've helped in this way are not only extremely grateful, they are forever loyal, and they repay the loan in so many ways that go far beyond just money. There is an emotional bond and friendship that lasts a lifetime. Think I'm kidding? Just ask one of my longtime team members, Sam Sawadogo, a pizza deliveryman from Burkina Faso who's been with me for more than a decade. He honored Angie and me beyond belief a few years ago when he named his son Melton. I'm planning on hiring Melton Sawadogo when he's ready to join the Domino's Pizza team!

■ PRACTICE FAMILY-STYLE COMMUNICATION

Angie and I run our business out of our home. We conduct our monthly manager meetings in our living room. We're incorporated, but we're not a corporation. We're a husband-and-wife team. With team members who have been with us for a decade, we feel like a family. So it comes naturally that we practice family-style communication. That means, essentially, that we don't dictate rules from some ivory tower or direct disciplinary action from a distance. Instead, we enjoy the genuine dialogue that exists with our team members, who take pride in working for Domino's Pizza.

Family-style communication means making yourself available to your team, which is why I give everyone my home and cell phone numbers and why we conduct meetings in which employees discuss profit and loss statements and marketing strategies while they're playing with a kitten who jumps at every movement. Every summer we invite our team to our house in Connecticut to rest, relax, and enjoy each other's company. I'm not suggesting that, if you are a hiring manager or business owner, the only way to make employees feel connected is to invite them to your home. I am suggesting that you *do* go out of your way to make them *feel* at home. When they feel comfortable and connected to you and your organization, I guarantee they're going to work harder to ensure the success of the enterprise.

AMERICAN DREAM EMPLOYEE: SCOTT HINSHAW

From $4.50 per Hour Assistant Manager to Executive Vice President

In 1980, Scott Hinshaw was going to school full-time as a freshman at the University of Wisconsin–Lacrosse. He was helping raise his little brother after his parents divorced and his father moved to Chicago. Scott was also managing a small pizzeria in town. He was 17.

After a year of this, Scott realized something: He loved the food business and believed he had discovered his niche. He told his parents he was going to quit school, move to Chicago, and pursue a career in the restaurant industry. He got a job at a Wendy's location and, due to his drive and passion, found himself managing a store less than a month later. Before his twenty-first birthday, Scott was supervising 20 Wendy's units in the Greater Chicago area and was on his way. The only problem: He wasn't happy. "I was successful, but the culture wasn't right for me. It didn't have the excitement and energy I wanted, so I left."

Excitement and energy were not exactly what he found at his next job: selling insurance at his father's company for a whopping $8,000 a year. One day he was leafing through *Time* magazine and read a story about Tom Monaghan and Domino's Pizza. The story featured a store manager in Washington, D.C., who was making $105,000 a year in salary and bonuses. "That was for me. In 1986, I found out that Domino's Pizza was coming to Chicago, and I wanted to be a part of it."

Scott proceeded to the newly opened regional office in Chicago and applied to be a supervisor, based on his extensive experience at Wendy's and the Wisconsin pizza shop. Domino's wasn't having any of it, however. "The regional director told me my previous experience didn't count for much. I'd have to start out in the assistant manager program, manage a store for a couple of years and if I was any good, maybe I'd get a chance to supervise someday, maybe in four or five years."

Undeterred, Scott left the office and went home, where he ripped out pages of his phone book with the addresses of the Domino's locations within driving distance of his apartment. Scott visited each store, introduced himself to all the managers, and asked them about their work at Domino's. Not only was he learning about the business, he was, in effect, scoping out his competition—these very managers would be competing with him for supervisory positions at Domino's if the company hired him. He liked the culture and the excitement at the stores, but also felt that he could outperform the managers he met. He returned to the regional office and confidently applied for an assistant manager's position, which meant he would be delivering pizzas and mopping floors, in addition to learning how to manage the "Domino's way." The job paid $4.50 an hour. He accepted.

"The growth was explosive in those days," Scott says. "There was a lot of opportunity, so I knew I could be successful once I got in. I love the business. I love the rush. I love making food and making people happy. I got such a thrill when customers would call the store to tell me this was the best pizza they ever had."

Scott's skill surprised and impressed his first manager, so much so that he had Scott run a shift after his second day on the job. What also impressed his boss was that Scott never seemed to leave the store. Even though he knew the company could pay him for only 40 hours of work a week, Scott stuck around as a "volunteer" for another 20 to 30 hours to learn as much as he could as quickly as he could. "For a long time, it was work, drive home, take a shower, sleep, go back to work . . . over and over and over again," Scott recalls. "I ate most of my meals in the car to and from my apartment."

Seven weeks later, well ahead of Domino's standard schedule, Scott was promoted to general manager and given his own store in Schaumburg, Illinois. Now he was making $350 a week and 20 percent of the store's profits. Within weeks,

(Continued)

(Continued)

sales jumped from $5,000 a week to $8,000. Scott and his team set five record weeks in the first two months. Five months later, again well ahead of Domino's promotion schedule, Scott was made a supervisor overseeing six stores in Racine and Kenosha, Wisconsin.

"I always thought that the opportunity to grow was there, and it still is," Scott says. "I believe that if you can outhustle, outenergy, outmove, and outwork people, you're going to go places." That's an understatement for Scott. From his supervisor role, Scott moved up in the system and around the country, building sales and building stores. He was named Corporate Operations Director of the Year in 1993 and, a year later, was promoted regional vice president for the Midwest.

Twenty years after joining the company and making $4.50 an hour, Scott was named vice president of Team USA, heading the operations of Domino's 500-plus company-owned stores. In 2007, he became executive vice president of that division; in 2008, he was named executive vice president of franchise operations and development for the company, responsible for working with 1,200 independent franchisees who own and operate 4,600 Domino's stores in the United States.

"This is a people business," Scott says. "It's all about 'team.' I love to compete. I love to fire people up and get them motivated. I love making customers happy with great product and killer service. Domino's is filled with hard-charging, bad-ass, water-walking team members who get after it every night. Anyone who comes in, no matter what level they start at, is going to find opportunities like mine if they work hard and are driven to succeed."

Chapter 9

Make the Rules of Promotion Public, and Put the Bottom 10 Percent of Your Employees "On Notice"

After more than 25 years of managing and leading employees, I have found one thing to be true: People want to succeed. It doesn't matter what the challenge is. Whether they're at work during the week or playing touch football on the weekends, people like to win. American culture thrives on competition, and beating the competition is a primary motivating force in American business. Succeeding at work takes many forms: It could mean mastering a difficult task, receiving accolades from the boss, or getting a raise and possibly a promotion. Your job as a manager is to help your team members succeed. When they win, you win.

When do you begin? Before you hire. Make sure you have a plan for your business and that you can articulate a vision for the future of your enterprise. What if you "only" operate a lawn care service and you cut other people's grass all day? Be the best at it! Think big! Plan to "own" entire neighborhoods! Inspire your crew to treat every lawn with individual care, because happy customers come back, and when they do, your business grows. This is what I say to my team about making pizzas. Each one has to be made with an individual customer in mind.

Articulate the vision for your company during the interview (using the situational interview process I outlined in Chapter 7). Hire only the people who understand the vision and buy into it.

I've found that incentives are a huge factor in driving the success of my team, from entry-level to management. Everyone likes to be recognized and rewarded for doing a good job. Incentives, as I pointed out in a list in Chapter 6, don't always have to be cash, although that is a very popular one, especially for minimum-wage employees. Parties, movie passes, concert tickets, clothing with your company's logo, a promise of promotion . . . these are all ideas for incentives.

In order for your team members to succeed, it is essential to define what *success* means for your operation, and more specifically, how it relates to their roles. In the case of the lawn care owner, success could be measured by increased efficiency in the operation: the number of lawns serviced per day without compromising quality of service or safety standards, for example. Success could be measured by the number of new customers generated in a specific neighborhood due to the team's great work on your existing customers' lawns. Success can be measured in any number of ways: The important thing is to define it for your team members.

■ PROVIDE YOUR EMPLOYEES WITH ROAD MAPS TO SUCCESS, BUT LET THEM DRIVE

Once you define success for your business, talk to your team members about their roles, and, together, define success for each individual. For some (maybe all) of your employees, success means more money and a promotion. Consider the promotion to be your employees' destination. Your job is to provide them with the road map. The road map should include skill levels you want them to reach, training courses you want them to complete, sales- or service-level milestones you want them to achieve, or experiences you want them to have. If you want your employees to complete a training class, the road map should include information on when and where the course is offered. If you want them to gain experience in a particular area of your business, chart out with them how you are going to give them the opportunity. As you work with an employee on his or her road map, you should keep two things in mind:

1. People will take different roads to their destination.
2. Your team members, not you, are responsible for driving their careers.

Let's take a look at what I mean:

1. Everybody's different, and we all read our road maps differently. Some of us like to get on the highway and move as fast as we can. Some of us like the journey and prefer the scenic route, taking our time getting to our destination. Career growth could mean continued success in an employee's existing job versus a promotion into another position. Certain team members in a lawn care service, for example, may not want to be promoted to a management or sales position . . . they might just want to cut and edge lawns, and that's okay. There are team members in my stores who want to concentrate on being the best pizza delivery people in Manhattan—they don't aspire to join our management training program, and that's okay, too. We provide our

better-performing delivery employees the equivalent of a promotion by letting them set their own schedules. They'll pick the busiest times, of course, because those are the best times to make more money. Other employees are like Jim Denburg. He wanted to get into the management training program as quickly as he could because he was focused on becoming a franchisee. Jim definitely took the superhighway to reach his destination.

2. Your job is to provide the road map and to help steer your team members in the right direction, but ultimately, their careers are up to them. Your employees have to choose their destination and decide how quickly they want to get there. You can provide them the vehicle, the fuel, the map, and even work to eliminate roadblocks . . . but they have to drive.

■ INSPIRE EMPLOYEES WITH THE OPPORTUNITIES THAT LIE BEFORE THEM

I like to tell my team members about great Domino's Pizza franchisees like Anthony Maestri, Emir Lopez, Rob Cookston, and Jim Denburg, all of whom worked for me before opening their own stores in Manhattan and all of whom started as minimum-wage employees delivering pizza. These real-life examples of successful store owners who all started out in hourly positions are proof of the opportunities that exist in this business. My managers also serve as proof: They started as delivery people and then worked their way up.

Another success story I often share is that of Arturo Ontiveros, who came to the United States in 1996 and joined our team in 2000. Arturo worked in a shoe factory in Mexico, but today is one of our top performers; he loves being an integral leader on our team and is someone who excels in delighting customers. He started as a delivery team member but has worked his way up to crew chief, ensuring that the store is prepped for the day, that fresh food is ready on the makeline, that the ovens are on, and that delivery team members are in the store ready to go. He is crucial to his store's success, and Arturo is participating in the American Dream.

In your business, it's important to tell the stories of employees, past and present, who started where your team members are now and who took advantage of the opportunities before them. Maybe you don't have that classic tale of the person who started in the mailroom and is now in the boardroom in your organization, but there are very likely examples of people who worked hard and advanced. Maybe the inspirational example is *you*. Don't be afraid to tell the story of how you came to be in the position you're in. Connecting with your team members and inspiring them can motivate them to achieve success.

■ MAKE THE RULES OF PROMOTION PUBLIC

One of the biggest mistakes managers make, aside from promoting the wrong people for the wrong reasons (because of seniority, for example, instead of productivity, or because they want to stop someone from complaining about their job, or because they want to give the problem to somebody else), is not communicating with their employees about what it takes to be considered for a promotion or a raise in the first place. If you will consider people for a higher-level position only after they've worked in their current position for at least a year, let them know that. If you require a specific set of skills to be mastered before a team member can go to the next level, let your employees know what those skills are and how they can go about learning them. Make sure all of your employees have the information; give everyone a fair shot . . . and may the best person win.

In my stores (as in all pizza shops), entry-level jobs include a number of tasks that people don't like to perform: cleaning the employee restroom, washing and sanitizing the pizza-making equipment, cleaning out the grease trap beneath the sink. They're unpleasant (sometimes very smelly!) jobs, but they have to be done. The newest team members are usually assigned those tasks, which shouldn't surprise anyone. How they tackle those tasks and the attitude they bring to the job will have a significant impact on how long they retain the assignment. Team members who do the job good-naturedly and take it seriously are going to be noticed and will get better assignments in the future. Moving from the back of the store to the front, or better yet, out into the street where they can interact directly with customers, is essentially a promotion that doesn't cost you anything but does wonders for an employee's morale.

Letting employees know that they have the ability to work themselves out of the unpleasant tasks to the better ones, and how they can do so, is crucial to determining how they will perform. Many restaurants will start employees out busing tables before they move them up to wait directly on customers. Movie theaters will have entry-level employees do the custodial jobs before they can move up to taking tickets, serving as ushers, or working concessions. Grocery stores will start new employees as baggers or assign them to gather carts from the parking lot before they can move up to running the register.

To become a manager at one of my pizza stores, you have to understand the basics of business and how to read and manage a profit and loss statement. You must have a demonstrated proficiency at working positively with people, customers and colleagues alike. You have to show you understand and demonstrate positive energy, hustle, integrity, and can lead in a high-pressure environment. You need strong communication skills. You must be proficient with all of the store's technology. You must understand marketing and operations. You need to be able to manage labor, address personnel challenges, and deal with problems that other people want you to own. (You must also know how to make great pizzas fast!)

When an employee lets me know that she wants to work her way into management, we sit down and I outline what skills she'll need and how she can go about mastering them. We outline an action plan and a rough timeline for accomplishing the tasks and gaining the knowledge and experience. I'll work with the manager in the store to ensure that he will provide her with the education, training, and opportunities to run various shifts. The rest would be up to her. In my franchise, I'm actually dealing with a "good" problem, and that is that there is a waiting list to get into my management program. I've had the same managers running my stores successfully for more than six years now. In order to provide my team of exceptional assistant managers the opportunity take over a store, there are currently three options: One of the current managers becomes a franchisee; I open another store; or one of my top assistant managers moves on to work for another franchisee. I never dreamed I would be in a position where my opportunities to promote team members would be limited! I keep them motivated by offering other challenges and providing cash and other incentives to continue delighting customers.

■ COACH, MEASURE, INSPECT, AND TRAIN—ESPECIALLY YOUR BEST PEOPLE

I believe that managers must do four things well in order to succeed in developing people and turning them into high-performance teams: coach, measure, inspect, and train.

Managers should put a greater emphasis on doing these things with employees who have the potential and want to be promoted to higher ranks in their organizations.

Coach

Managers can't do everything. They have to rely on their employees to get things accomplished, whether it's assembling a product, bagging groceries, cutting lawns, or making sales calls. Like coaches on the sideline who rely on their players to make plays, managers have to depend on their employees. I believe in positive coaching by building self-esteem, not by heavy-handed criticism or intimidation. You need to make employees *want* to achieve for you. Inspire them with coaching, offer them tips on how to improve their performance, and provide the necessary feedback they need to get better. If an employee is not getting a task done right, don't make negative assumptions or presume that the employee is goofing off or isn't competent. It might be a simple need for more coaching to handle the task. Let your employees know what they need to do to meet your standards; then help them get there.

Measure

Employees need benchmarks to know that they're meeting your expectations. At Domino's Pizza, we measure *everything*. We measure how long phone orders take, how long it takes to make a pizza and get it into the oven, how fast we get an order out the door. We measure the distances from our stores to our customers' doors. We often time our pizza makers and train them to get faster. We measure sales and service performance against yesterday, last week, last month, and last year; we measure it against our neighboring stores and franchisees and against our competition. There are major components of your business that should be measured, from sales to workdays lost due to accident or injury, from product returns to customer complaints. Use these and other measures to help your team understand and achieve your objectives.

Inspect

Many people have heard the phrase, "You don't get what you *expect* unless you *inspect*," and it is absolutely true. You won't truly know how your employees handle customer calls unless you pose as a customer yourself or record the telephone interaction. Instead of recording customer interactions, I prefer to call my stores directly, with the store manager present in the same room with me, and go through the entire pizza ordering process. This allows me and the manager to see how quickly the phones are being answered and whether the person on the other end is enthusiastic and nice. We can determine whether the customer service rep is offering specials, answering questions, or engaging in suggestive selling. Likewise, we call our competition and do the same thing so that we can benchmark. We share what we find with our team members—specifically to help them get better, not to punish them if they don't get it right. At the stores, I time my pizza makers to see how fast they make an order. I routinely and randomly open boxes of orders ready to go out the door to do a quality check against our standards. If a pizza doesn't meet our standards, I won't hesitate to point out the problem, toss the pizza out, and ask the pizza maker to remake the order. If you manage employees who work at off-site locations, visit the job site and watch from a distance to see how they're progressing, then make yourself known and offer suggestions for improvement. If you have an office job, get out of the office and visit your employees at their workstations. If you are a manager of a retail shop, spend time on the floor to see how your team members are greeting and treating customers.

Train

This is the foundation for any new employee or a team member who is moving into a new position, laterally or as a promotion. Management guru Ken Blanchard developed a learning grid to best explain how to teach an employee a skill. In its essence, it is a four-step process: (1) The employee watches you demonstrate the task to see how it's done. (2) You and the employee do the task together to ensure the employee understands the basic principles. (3) You watch the employee do the task on his or her own and offer coaching and tips for getting it done. (4) The employee does the task on his or her own until eventually becoming proficient enough to teach it to somebody else using the same four-step process. While we didn't have a name for it (other than *training*) until Blanchard coined the phrase "learning grid," this is exactly how we've been teaching the art and skill of pizza making at Domino's for almost 50 years.

■ REWARD YOUR BEST PERFORMERS

I love rewarding team members who excel at their jobs. Throughout the year I will offer up challenges, set the bar higher, and encourage my employees to meet or beat the goals I set. When they do, they are rewarded with cash or some other incentive. Sometimes I'll make the challenge a competition between the stores. Sometimes I'll challenge an individual store team to meet a goal. Sometimes I'll just target a certain group of my employees (pizza makers, for example) or a particular individual who needs to improve or who has proven worthy of new opportunities. In every case, I'll make the challenge known, communicate it as a SMAC (specific, measurable, achievable, compatible) objective, and offer the reward.

I like to come up with unique ideas for challenges, based on the individual involved. In 2007, for example, I offered a team member a chance to get into our management training program (which was a promotion that came with an increase in salary) if she would take a multiweek, city-sanctioned food safety certification course, because knowing what the city looks for when it sends health inspectors into our stores is vitally important. Even more important is knowing how to improve on our process to ensure the safety and quality of the food we sell to our customers. Our team member took the course and passed the test, and she was rewarded with a promotion, a raise, and a bonus. She then shared her knowledge with the rest of our team.

■ PUT THE BOTTOM 10 PERCENT OF YOUR EMPLOYEES "ON NOTICE"

When managers look at their team members objectively, they will usually find that they can name a select few who are their go-to people: the ones they can always rely on to meet or beat expectations. They're the ones who come in early to prepare for the day or stay late whenever there is a major deadline looming. They're the ones who always show up on time, ready to get to work, and who always work the shifts for which they're scheduled.

Likewise, managers can almost always think of the team members who cause the most consternation: the ones who don't show up on time or are inconsistent with their approach to the job. If managers are asked to rank their employees, they probably could easily identify the top 10 percent and the bottom 10 percent.

Much of this book is about inspiring all of your employees to want to be in your top 10 percent, but the bottom 10 percent is a painful reality that business owners and managers must address. This is a controversial concept, and Ford Motor Company was publicly criticized some years ago when it announced to its employee base that it would rank employees by job classification with the intent on cutting out the bottom 10 percent from its payroll. However, I'm not talking about identifying your bottom 10 percent as a cost-cutting measure. Instead, I'm suggesting putting them on notice and letting them know that they must face the facts: They must improve their performance or risk being replaced when a better candidate comes along. In my experience, many employees appreciate knowing where they stand and ask how they can improve. When they do that, we work with them to move them up into the middle 80 percent.

A team member in your bottom 10 percent is not necessarily a deadbeat or a problem employee (although some of them very likely are, like the guys in my first store who mistreated customers, were unreliable, and stole money from me). Instead, a bottom 10 percenter might be a team member who needs more coaching or who might need to be placed in a different role within your organization, one that provides a better fit. If an employee is part of your bottom 10 percent due to *attitude*, that's a different situation. Attitude is more important than skill, and a person's attitude is infectious in your business. If positive energy coaching can't fix a bad attitude, it's time to let that bad apple go.

■ GREAT LEADERS TAKE ON BIG RESPONSIBILITIES

Some employees think that a promotion means more money for less work. Isn't that the image many people have of the boss? In my experience, it's the opposite. Yes, the rewards for managers or business owners are greater, but so are the responsibilities and the risks that come with the job. I like to find the people on my team who are constantly looking for more responsibility, who want to tackle more challenges, who want to make a major positive impact on my business.

In the Foreword to this book, Domino's CEO David Brandon makes the point that he wants to benchmark everything about Domino's Pizza (from market share to employee turnover) against the *best*, not against the average.

Find the people in your organization who demonstrate strong leadership characteristics. (Here's a hint: The first place to look is among your top 10 percent.) They are the people who can be groomed for greater things. And don't hesitate for a moment to look among your entry-level and minimum-wage team members for the future leaders of your company. After all, that's what this whole book is about!

Chapter

10

How to Give Feedback and Conduct Performance Appraisals

No matter what your title is, you are not "the boss." Your customers are. Your job is to represent your customers to your employees. Every business exists to serve clients or customers, to meet a need or fulfill a desire. Every customer has choices and every business has competitors. There are other organizations out there (restaurants, car washes, movie theaters, pizza shops, lawn care services, grocery stores) that want your customers, and it doesn't take much for customers to leave you these days. It is simple cause and effect: More competition means more choice for customers, which means you have to get better by working harder and smarter.

As the customer's "inside" representative, it is your responsibility to ensure your frontline employees understand what it takes to delight the people you serve. The more delighted customers you have, the more your business will grow and the more opportunity there will be for your team members to benefit from the business's success.

Remember what I said in Chapter 4 about customers. I tell my managers not to run their stores to make *me* happy, because I don't buy many pizzas from them. They need to run their stores to make their *customers* happy. Even though I own the stores, our customers are the ones who decide if I get "fired" for not meeting or exceeding their expectations.

■ PERFORMANCE EVALUATIONS FOR YOUR FRONTLINE EMPLOYEES ARE ESSENTIAL

We put extra emphasis on training our customer service reps and our delivery team members because they are the ones who directly interact with our customers. We also ensure that we evaluate their performance on a regular basis. It's not uncommon for major corporations or office-based businesses to do performance evaluations, of course, but for smaller companies that rely on minimum wage and hourly team members, the thought of doing performance appraisals might seem foreign. Why take the time to do a performance evaluation for a minimum-wage position? Performance appraisals are time-consuming and costly, and we're just talking about entry-level employees who don't stick around anyway, right?

Wrong. Your frontline employees are crucial to your business—mine certainly are to my business. Once you hire them, train them, and put your employees in front of your customers, how could you *not* evaluate their performance? How can your team members improve if you don't provide them with the feedback they need? How can you build them from entry-level team members to future long-term contributors without making the investment in assessing their skills? You can't. Performance appraisals are essential.

You can evaluate your entry-level team members effectively once you've communicated your expectations:

➤ Punctuality
➤ Reliability

- ➤ Dress and appearance on the job
- ➤ Attitude and demeanor
- ➤ Friendliness
- ➤ Efficiency
- ➤ Ability to meet deadlines
- ➤ Core competency and job skills
- ➤ Customer service
- ➤ Teamwork

For my delivery team members, we created a checklist of what constitutes "the perfect delivery." The list was generated during a team meeting in which a group of delivery experts suggested what should be on it, then debated and refined it until we came up with the final list that follows. That list includes everything from how employees should dress to how they interact with the customer, from how they ride their bikes to how they manage money. We then use this checklist during our performance appraisals. Below is the Perfect Delivery checklist, followed by the Delivery Expert Evaluation. Both are very specific to my business, but you can use these as models for outlining the important elements of your frontline employees' roles in your company and as factors in how you can evaluate them.

The Perfect Delivery

- ➤ Outfitted with complete uniform.
- ➤ Proper hygiene.
- ➤ Carry only one order at a time, two with manager's okay.
- ➤ Leave the store with no more than $20.
- ➤ Have the *complete* order with you (pizza, beverages, side items, extras).
- ➤ Use a HeatWave delivery bag that is *hot*.
- ➤ Bring napkins for a business delivery.

- ➤ Call out the time out the door loud and clear.
- ➤ Hold the pizza level during the delivery.
- ➤ Remember: You are carrying someone's food.
- ➤ Hustle to your delivery.
- ➤ No riding on the sidewalk—be respectful.
- ➤ Carry several promotional flyers and distribute them.
- ➤ Introduce yourself at the customer's door.
- ➤ Speak clearly and with deference.
- ➤ Smile!
- ➤ Make eye contact.
- ➤ Count out the customer's change.
- ➤ Give a sincere "thank you for ordering."
- ➤ Tell the customers that we appreciate their business.
- ➤ Hustle back to the store.
- ➤ Call out the delivery time.
- ➤ Check back in.
- ➤ Put the money and receipt from the order into your locked drop box.

During Delivery Expert Evaluations, our managers rank our employees on a three-point scale: Excellent, Good, and Need to Improve (NTI). The goal is to receive an Excellent rating, of course, but Good is all right, especially if the team member is committed to doing better. A rating of NTI is typically given to someone who is in our bottom 10 percent. For us, we try to determine whether the rating is due to a lack of training and experience or attitude. NTI won't get you fired, necessarily, but it will put you on notice.

Whenever a team member is rated a Need to Improve and the reasons are not due to a negative attitude, we will work with him or her and set up a timeline for improvement. After 30 to 60 days, we will reevaluate the employee to determine whether that employee has made progress. You will likely find that many employees who are performing poorly will appreciate the feedback and will try to get better. Some will quit, and the rare few will wait for you to fire them. Domino's CEO Dave Brandon has lectured on that kind of personality during franchise meetings. "Look for the team members who have 'quit' but haven't left yet. They are weighing you down and taking good performers with them. Get them out sooner rather than later and save yourself grief down the line."

All of our performance evaluations are documented in writing. We include the name of the person being evaluated and the person conducting the evaluation. After the evaluation is complete, we ask the employee to sign the document and date it. (This helps us maintain a complete record of the individual employee so that we can chart his or her progress. Documented performance appraisals also offer protection in today's litigious society.) We also give the employees a chance on the form itself to let us know what they think of the evaluation by telling us whether they agree or disagree with the score they received. Our evaluation checklist for delivery team members follows. This can also be used as a template for evaluating the crucial components of your employees' performance. You'll see that instead of simply noting items like punctuality or appearance, we define them for our employees so that there is no misinterpretation about the evaluation.

Delivery Expert Evaluation

All are rated on a scale of Excellent, Good, or Need to Improve.

Self-Presentation
- ➤ Punctuality: ready to start work at scheduled time
- ➤ Appearance: in complete uniform and neatly groomed
- ➤ Hustle (motivation and attitude)
- ➤ Understands and complies with company policies
- ➤ Ability to adapt and work effectively under pressure

Setup

➤ Bicycle cleaned and mechanically ready for start of shift

➤ Pizza bag selected and cleaned

Delivery

➤ In and out of the store within 60 seconds during rushes

➤ Reads order slip: verifies address, checks price and number of items in order

➤ Calls customer with any questions about order

➤ Calls time out the door

➤ Runs to and from the bicycle

➤ Makes frequent drops in drop box (with currency in "bank ready" condition)

➤ Verifies late deliveries from customer's phone

➤ Uses trip sheet (a record of which employee delivered to which addresses)

➤ Consistently checks out within $1.00 (cash compared to receipts)

➤ Familiar with delivery area; delivers efficiently without getting lost

➤ Obeys traffic laws; does not ride on sidewalks

➤ Delivery person not target of customer complaints

Miscellaneous

This category could be rated "not applicable," depending on the person being evaluated.

➤ Box tops glued to boxes and boxes folded

➤ Driver table, routing area, and back room kept clean

➤ Does not go on break without manager approval

➤ Does not eat in front of store

➤ Stays busy in store helping to clean and prep store during slow periods

The evaluation form includes a section called "Target Areas for Improvement," in which the manager and employee can document specific issues, such as punctuality, attitude, or lack of helping out during slow times. Finally, the employee signs the document after noting his or her acknowledgment of this sentence: "I have read and discussed this evaluation with my manager and I (agree) or (disagree)." If a team member disagrees with an evaluation, the manager will not hesitate to contact me and, together, the three of us (the employee, the manager, and I) will have a private meeting to see if we can come to a resolution of the disagreement. Thankfully, this has rarely happened, but it is important for employees to know that they do have an appeal process if needed. In these situations, I listen to both sides and offer an idea for resolution. It is imperative that I remain objective, but that I make recommendations I believe are in the best interests of the real boss, our customers.

My friend Tony Osani, who owns several Domino's Pizza stores in and around Huntsville, Alabama, provided me with some insight into how he defines the critical job skills in his stores. His new-employee orientation book (excerpts are included in Chapter 11) outlines for team members five primary general responsibilities and six technical skills on which they will be evaluated. This list is a good model for most entry-level positions. With the exception of the few that are clearly Domino's-specific, you can use them as a guide to develop your own list for employees.

General Responsibilities

Attitude and teamwork. Understands and follows all instructions as directed by the management team or area supervisor. Excellence in these areas would be the team member's attitude toward position and other team members. This will include teamwork with others in the store and following all safety and security policies to help in keeping all team members safe. This should also include being able to count on the team members to do their job (once trained) with little or no direction during the rush, to include helping out in the store when there are no deliveries ready to go.

Customer service attitude. Team member has the ability to listen and communicate with our customers on the telephone and in person. Team member has a positive attitude toward taking care of the customer. This includes being able to respond in the appropriate manner in order to resolve minor service issues for customers without a poor attitude in doing so. Team member delivers orders in priority, the oldest first. Team member takes complete orders to the customer and quickly reports and takes care of incorrectly made orders or forgotten items.

Attendance. Team member can be counted on to report for scheduled shifts and to help the store in being prepared to conquer the *rush*.

Punctuality. Team member arrives for work on time, in complete uniform, and ready to work.

Hustle. Team member completes task in a quick, efficient manner without sacrificing quality or service to the customer and helps the store in achieving service goals.

Technical Skills

Safety and security. Team member follows all safety and security policies. This includes but is not limited to: callbacks, making drops after each delivery, turning insurance in on time, reporting all incidents to management, driving safely and courteously, and wearing a seatbelt at all times.

Image. Team member *always* meets image and appearance standards. Helps the store in achieving top-notch image through sanitation and keeping his or her work area clean. Team member's vehicle is always clean and in good repair. Team member uses a lit car sign on all deliveries where applicable.

Phone-handling ability. Team member can courteously take and record a customer's order within two minutes. Team member knows all current specials and strives to always give the customer the best deal.

Pizza-making ability. Team member can make quality product using the Edge Stretch Method and proper portioning. Team member has ability to properly train new pizza makers on product quality and proper portioning. Team member knows and follows handling guidelines for deep dish, thin crust, chicken wings, and all bread products.

Routing and knowledge of area. Safe Delivery Specialist has expert knowledge of the delivery area and can independently route orders together to give the best service possible to the customer.

Teamwork with other stores. Team member is willing to help out at *any* store when asked by management.

■ EXPECT DEGREES OF IMPROVEMENT FROM YOUR TEAM MEMBERS

When you are providing a performance evaluation and are working with someone who needs help in certain areas, don't expect a full turnaround overnight. Give employees incremental goals they feel they can accomplish, such as "try to get 10 percent better" at whatever the task is. (For my stores, it might be improving their pizza-making speed by five seconds, for example.) Asking team members to get incrementally better at something will not intimidate them. I got this idea from a book I read some years ago called *The Plus 10% Game* by Mark Rosenberger. Rosenberger suggests that someone will feel that 10 percent improvement is attainable, and as your team members reach their personal incremental goals, their confidence will improve along with their skills.

The goal of a performance appraisal is not punishment; the goal is improvement. You want your team members to succeed, because when they do, you do. It's an opportunity to give your team members a pat on the back, catch them doing something right, and reinforce the behavior you're looking for. Approach every evaluation as an opportunity to help your employees shine!

AMERICAN DREAM EMPLOYEE: ASI SHEIKH

Executive Vice President Started Delivering Pizzas for $3.65 an Hour

Asi Sheikh learned about the importance of work ethic and personal sacrifice from his father, who taught those lessons from more than 10,000 miles away.

Asi was born in Pakistan. When he was four years old, his father took a job as a college professor in Fort Collins, Colorado, leaving his family behind. While he returned to Pakistan every summer, Professor Sheikh worked hard in the United States until he had enough money to bring his family to this country permanently. It took seven years. The family eventually settled in Rock Springs, Wyoming, where Asi's dad was then working for West Wyoming College. During those years, Asi learned about sacrifice and commitment—lessons he instills today as executive vice president of Domino's company-owned stores.

But Asi wasn't planning on a career at Domino's Pizza, nor was his mother, who pushed him to pursue a professional, "respectable" job in banking. Asi discovered Domino's Pizza quite by accident in 1984; and, although he didn't know it at the time, his discovery would lead him to break his mother's heart.

"In 1984 I was a freshman at the University of North Carolina–Greensboro," Asi says. "Back then, *Dynasty* was the biggest show on TV—everybody watched it. A bunch of students were in the dorm dining hall, watching the show, and somebody ordered pizza from Domino's. I saw this guy walk in looking pretty cool—and saw that he got a pretty good tip. I figured he had to be making some good money. The next day I went to the store and applied for a job."

At the time, Asi was interested in earning enough money for gas to get from Greensboro to Atlanta, where his then girlfriend was attending college. He was hired as a driver making $3.65 plus tips. During his four years at UNC–Greensboro, he stayed with Domino's and learned the ins and outs of daily operations, although he turned down requests to become an assistant manager at the store. "I was studying to be a banker," he says. "I was not going to become a Domino's store manager." He set his sights on wearing a suit and tie and carrying a briefcase when he graduated, not on wearing a pizza store uniform.

Asi graduated and got a job at North Carolina National Bank as an assistant branch manager, making a salary of $26,700. He left a week later. "I was good with numbers, which is why I went into banking," he says. "After doing a bit of calculation, I realized I was actually making more money delivering pizzas than I was as an assistant branch manager at NCNB. Besides, I just didn't 'feel it' at the bank. There was no excitement. And while they promised me that I could be a branch manager in six months, making $35,000 a year, I just had to leave."

Asi initially took a four-week leave of absence, citing personal reasons. He left for Brooklyn, where his family now lived, and spent some time soul-searching. While in Brooklyn, Asi walked into a Domino's Pizza shop on Avenue X and applied to be a driver. "I thought I'd deliver for a few days, make a few bucks, then head back to Greensboro," Asi says. When the manager realized Asi could also make pizzas well and had four years of experience in store operations, he offered him a job as an assistant manager making $500 a week. "I said yes, even though I was still only planning to be there for a few weeks. But three weeks later, I was offered a job as a general manager of my own store in Brooklyn. I accepted, but I didn't want to tell my mother."

(Continued)

(Continued)

Asi's mom, of course, noticed that he wasn't packing his bags to return to NCNB in Greensboro. In an emotional conversation, he told her that banking was not where he wanted to be. "I told her not to worry, I was going to make it. It was difficult. I broke her heart."

She's gotten over it.

Asi excelled in his first manager's job, raising sales and setting records. He became known as a turnaround specialist in the franchise that operated the stores in Brooklyn. He would take over a store, improve its operations, customer service, and sales, and then he would be moved to another store to attempt the same feat. He managed five different stores in his first year. "I was lucky that people liked me," Asi says. "I was able to build great teams in the stores because people trusted me. In these markets, our hourly employees were 100 percent immigrants, and I could relate to them. What is most important to them is respect and trust. Every time I would go into a store I would repeat to them something I got from (renowned college football coach) Lou Holtz. Coach Holtz says, 'Do what's right. And do the best you can do.' That's all I asked of them, and that's what I ask of them today."

While his individual stores were succeeding, the market as a whole was failing. The corporation came in and purchased the stores from the franchisee in 1994. The corporate leadership first asked Asi to become a training director, but in 1995 promoted him to corporate operations director, overseeing 37 stores in Brooklyn, the Bronx, Queens, and Long Island.

"I didn't realize how extremely fragile we were in these markets, how close to closing we were," Asi recalls. "I just kept focusing ahead and trying to build a strong team."

The market was losing $1 million a year, but Asi knew that if the 37 stores, which were then averaging $9,000 a week in sales, could average $10,000 by the end of the year, they would turn a profit . . . of one dollar. That became their goal. In April of 1996, sales were down 11.4 percent, and things seemed bleak, but Asi didn't give up. "One dollar profit" became a rallying cry among managers and team members at meetings. By December, sales had reversed and were up 11.5 percent, a 22.9 percent swing! Domino's decided not to close the stores, and they have flourished ever since. Asi went on to earn four Corporate Operations Director of the Year awards. By 2001, the now 56-store market was averaging sales of $20,000 a week and returning to the company annual profits of $6.5 million.

In 2008, Asi was asked to lead the 500-plus company-owned stores throughout the United States. He plans to lead them the way he did in New York.

"For me, everything is personal. I believe in relying on other people to make things better and creating a culture built on trust and commitment. I approach this business by asking my team three questions: Can I trust you? Are you committed? Do you trust me? I want people to get up every morning, put on their uniform and say to themselves, 'I want to be great.' I tell my team that they should never lower their standards, because I'm sure not going to lower mine."

Chapter 11

Sample Philosophy / Vision Statements, Training Tools, Forms, and More

Throughout this book, I've provided you with a number of ideas on how to turn entry-level, minimum-wage employees into a high-performance, customer-focused team. I've shared things that I do, the lessons I've learned in more than 25 years of hiring and leading teams. In this chapter, I'm going to share many of the forms and documents we use to help our team members at Domino's Pizza New York. I'm also including a number of pieces from my friends throughout the world, all of whom run incredibly successful Domino's franchises. There are 17 separate documents here, and most are very Domino's-specific, but they can be adapted for use in any business, including yours. You should break down your business to this same level of detail. It will not only help you identify the key components of your operations, it will help you identify strengths and weaknesses, and most important, it will help you communicate to your employees. I've divided the chapter into four sections:

1. "Focus Your Employees on What's Important." This section provides ideas and inspiration for creating and communicating a vision for your company.

2. "Building a Team." This section contains some intriguing ideas from Down Under on how to turn a group of individuals into a cohesive, single-minded team.

3. "Employee Attitude and Behavior." This section addresses how different franchises throughout the country communicate expectations, set standards and hold team members accountable for their actions in the workplace.

4. "Exceptional Customer Service." As the cornerstone of any retail business, customer service deserves a separate section, to reinforce the concepts discussed in Chapter 5. This section comes primarily from my franchise.

■ SECTION 1. FOCUS YOUR EMPLOYEES ON WHAT'S IMPORTANT: EXAMPLES OF MISSION/VISION STATEMENTS

Domino's Pizza Enterprises (DPE) is the largest Domino's master franchise in the world. Based in Brisbane, Australia, DPE operates its own company stores and sells franchises. The company is publicly traded on the Australian stock exchange. It is the leading pizza company in both Australia and New Zealand, and Domino's Pizza Enterprises operates stores in the Netherlands, Belgium, and France. At the end of 2008, Domino's Pizza Enterprises comprised more than 750 stores in five countries.

Don Meij, while attending college to become a schoolteacher, began working in a pizza shop near Brisbane in the early 1980s and quickly decided that pizza sauce was in his veins (a key attribute of Domino's Pizza people worldwide, as you've learned by now). In short order, Don excelled at managing a store, and he was named the International Manager of the Year while still in his early twenties. He became a franchisee and eventually merged his stores with

the Australian master franchise in order to become its CEO—
which, in his case, also means chief *enthusiasm* officer. A few
years ago, he was one of the very few individuals inducted
into the Domino's Pizza Chairman's Circle Hall of Fame, an
honor personally bestowed on individuals by David Brandon, chairman of Domino's Pizza, Inc.—all of this before the
age of 35.

In the course of writing this book, I asked Don to share with
me some of philosophies he holds and some of the materials
that Domino's Pizza Enterprises employees receive during the
course of their employment with the company. He sent me a
copy of a booklet they distribute to all new store employees,
called "What We Believe." With his permission, I'm reprinting
the content of this booklet here, because it aligns so closely
with what I believe. It is a remarkable example of sharing a
vision and communicating a culture to all who join it.

WHAT WE BELIEVE

Our Vision: No. 1 in People. No. 1 in Pizza.
Domino's is not just unlike any other pizza company, it's
unlike any other business. It can take up to 80 people to run
a Domino's store, unlike other chains which need as few as
8. That's why having a strong team is so important. We need
them to be 110 percent motivated, working in unison and constantly improving. Being the best at treating, training and
incentivizing our people is our secret to being No. 1 in pizza.

Our Mission: Sell more pizza, have more fun.
If there's a pizza being sold, we want it to be a Domino's pizza.
We are a volume business, not a niche business. Demand can
surge at any time. Dominoids don't dread the "rush," they
thrive on it. It's like a sport; we love competing within our
teams, against other teams, and against ourselves to continually set new personal bests. Riding the rush should be the
most fun part of the job.

WHAT WE BELIEVE: THE BIG EIGHT
(DOWNLOADABLE)

1. **Treat people as you'd like to be treated.**
   Treating people with respect isn't just good business, it's good manners. We encourage fun but never at the expense of customers or another team member. We play to win but never gloat. We treat every $10 customer as a potential $1,000 a year customer—if we never lose one, sales can only go up.

2. **Produce the best for less.**
   Is a full-color box in the best interests of the customer? Probably not. Is using real chicken instead of compressed chicken? Yes. We never stop questioning every aspect of our business. It's not about cost cutting; it's about making the right decision for the customer. Because that's the right decision for the business.

3. **Measure, manage, and share what's important.**
   We can measure almost everything in our business—but we choose not to. Analyze, but don't overanalyze. Only measure what you need to know and are prepared to manage now. Pick five to seven things, max, to measure, learn, make improvements, share your learnings, then move on to measure and manage something else. That's how we get better.

4. **Think big and grow.**
   Dominoids believe you can't shrink your way to success and that standing still is the same as going backward. If you want to fit into the Domino's culture you must always think big, have a passion for growth and an insatiable appetite for personal and team improvement.

5. **Incentivize what you want to change.**
   You can get a horse to do what you want using a carrot or a stick. Domino's prefers using the carrot whenever possible. Everyone is motivated by "What's in it for me?". It's human nature. We love being competitive; it bonds teams, makes working at Domino's fun, and lets us measure and fully reward improvements.

6. **Set the bar high, train, never stop learning.**
Getting better at saucing, shaving seconds off delivery times, taking orders more efficiently. These are
the kinds of things that drive Domino's forward.
Dominoids want to train and want to be trained. If
you're not interested in getting better, what are you
doing here?

7. **Promote from within.**
Many of Domino's most senior people started as
drivers or on the makeline. Succeeding here is in no
small part down to "getting the culture." Dominoids
are already in the zone; outsiders aren't. And because
we attract such diverse people we also have a wealth
of unexpected skills and experience in our midst. Tap
into it. It sends great signals to others of how everyone can progress.

8. **We are not ordinary, we are exceptional.**
What sort of person gets fanatical about two-swirl
saucing or turns the busiest times into the most fun
times? Dominoids, that's who. We count pepperoni in
our sleep. We take pride in being different. Domino's
is exceptional for one reason only: We have exceptional people working in exceptional teams who are
obsessed with continual improvement. That's us.

➤ Ten Things

My first boss was a man named Frank Meeks. He was an inspiration to me, and he remains an icon within the community of
Domino's Pizza. Frank, who passed away in 2002, was the first
franchisee conducted into the Chairman's Circle Hall of Fame

by Domino's CEO David Brandon. One of the things Frank's franchise was known for was his relentless focus on (some might say obsession with) the basics of product, service, and image. In the 1980s, he drafted what he called the "Ten Things" that comprise the foundation of store management. You can use this as an outline to identify the 10 basics of your business.

THE 10 BASICS OF STORE MANAGEMENT (DOWNLOADABLE)

1. **Service.** The customer is the boss. The job of every team member is to go way out of our way to *impress* every customer. This means we must meet our goal of 30-minute or less delivery and do it in such a friendly and ethical manner that customers will feel good about doing business with us. When we do not come through, we must always happily honor our guarantees.

2. **Product.** Our goal is to deliver a hot, tasty, high-quality pizza every time. To do this we must manage our dough every minute to ensure proper proofing, slap the dough correctly, put on the correct amount of sauce, cheese, and toppings, and properly maintain our ovens. When we do not come through for the customer, we must happily honor our product guarantee.

3. **Cost management.** We do want to make big profits, but we must do so by raising sales and controlling waste—not by cheating the customers or our team members.

4. **Training.** We must provide our team at all levels with the best training classes available on a regular basis. The best training, however, is day by day, on the job doing the best we can to better ourselves and our fellow team members.

5. **Image.** The feeling that Domino's Pizza generates to customers and potential customers concerning our

---

company is very important. Image can be enhanced or defaced by store cleanliness, appearance, and attitude of team members, service, product, advertising, price, and press articles. We must strive to go beyond just the expected in all of these areas.

6. **Cleanliness/maintenance.** A clean, well-maintained store is the best reflection of pride we have in our operation. We must take no shortcuts—neither time or financial—to ensure a clean, well-maintained company.

7. **Security and safety.** The safety of our work environment and our employees is the manager's most important responsibility.

8. **Paperwork.** Daily, weekly, period paperwork must be completed in a timely manner and be legible, accurate, and stored for easy access.

9. **Fun.** Do not get in a routine! Come to work every day to serve the customer and have fun. We set the tone for our customers and our fellow team members.

10. **Sales-building.** If you consistently do all of the preceding, sales will go up. If not, you must advertise to replace lost customers. Advertising, hanging sales fliers on doors, and so on can help a great store become greater.

FROM THE ARCHIVES OF DOMINO'S PIZZA TEAM WASHINGTON. To customize this document, download this form to your hard drive from www.hiretheamericandream.com. The document can then be opened, edited, and printed using Microsoft Word or another popular word processing application.

➤ The Two-Minute Drill: Preparing the Work Area for Action

I try to instill a sense of urgency at my stores—not only about pizza delivery, but about making sure that hustle is a central attribute of every team member. I expect that any of my team members can go into their store, check out a variety of key things, and to do it in two minutes. Following is the checklist they review during these "two-minute drills."

THINGS TO CHECK (DOWNLOADABLE)

Front of store
➤ Clean, organized, and "customer-ready."
➤ Towels and soap at sink.
➤ Menu holders filled outside and in front of counter.
➤ Napkins in napkin holder.
➤ Sidewalk and customer area clean.

Phone counter, cut table, hot rack
➤ Utensils clean and sanitized.
➤ No rags without sanitizer solution; use test strips.
➤ Upselling message in use.

Pizza makeline, dough table
➤ Thermometers working; equipment at 33 to 38 degrees.
➤ All food properly stored in makeline.
➤ No expired dough.
➤ All dough trays covered tightly.

Hand sink, bathroom
➤ Paper towels and soap at sink.
➤ Toilet tissue in bathroom.
➤ Trash can covered.

Back of store
➤ Cleaning supplies on bottom shelf only.
➤ Prep table clean; can opener clean.
➤ No storage on floor; use dunnage racks.

Walk-in cooler
➤ All dough in walk-in covered tightly.
➤ All food products dated.
➤ No expired dough or food.
➤ No personal food items in walk-in.

Things to remember
➤ Use of *heightened time awareness* (call out load times, oven time, out-the-door times, and delivery times).

> ➤ Name tags, belts, proper pants, shaven, haircut, perfect uniform.
> ➤ Aprons worn by all team members on makeline.
> ➤ Wash hands before assisting on makeline.
> ➤ Drivers make drops after each run (no more than $20 on driver, *including* personal money).

◼ SECTION 2. BUILDING A TEAM

➤ Strategies for Building a Strong Team

There are many things I love about Domino's Pizza. One of them is the great body of successful franchisees all over the world who don't hesitate to help you when you ask. It's reciprocal, too. In the past several years, Angie and I have hosted managers and franchisees from around the country and all over the world. Likewise, I've been invited to speak to franchisees and managers in the United States, Canada, Australia, England, Holland, France, Mexico, and the Caribbean. I love to share best practices and secrets to success. In that spirit of sharing, I once again asked Don Meij, the chief enthusiasm officer of Domino's Pizza Enterprises, to share some of the things DPE does to make its team so remarkably successful. He sent along his entire management training book. I particularly like this section, called "Strategies for Building a Team." As with any team-oriented organization, sports metaphors abound in this section of the DPE handbook for store managers.

STRATEGIES FOR BUILDING A TEAM
(DOWNLOADABLE)

Get to know your teammates.
The more you understand about a person, the easier it is to accept his or her differences. It's easy to be critical and negative about a person you don't understand. Take time and listen to the person with whom you're having trouble. Try to see through his or her eyes. If you can do that, your feelings toward that person almost always improve.

Give positive feedback to your teammates whenever you get the chance.
Simple statements like "good tackle," "nice try," "great job," "super," or "I knew you could do it" help build strong, positive relationships. Be positive and supportive verbally to your fellow players, and avoid the critical, negative feedback. In other words, get into the habit of saying things to your teammates that build them up and avoid saying things that put them down. This is particularly true in adversity. Remember, everyone has the tendency to retreat into him- or herself and protect "number one" when things get tough. When you're part of a team, that strategy spells trouble for you and everyone else. Work extra hard to be supportive, positive, and constructive with your team during times of adversity. By helping them, you end up helping yourself.

Give 100 percent effort in practice and work hard on your weaknesses.
In our business, you can't prepare for the rush during the rush. The time to practice making pizzas fast is . . . every time there is a pizza to make. Being able to perform the job perfectly when it's slow prepares the team to be able to provide great service and pizzas when it's really busy. Working hard to improve yourself and giving full effort is a powerful team unifier. When you are dedicated and committed, you encourage others to do likewise by example. Never underestimate the power of your example in building team spirit.

Both negativism and positivism are highly contagious.
Don't be fooled into believing that your negative attitude isn't

affecting your team. Negativism can spread through a team like a disease. Carefully guard what you think and say. Start an epidemic of enthusiasm and excitement on your team by being optimistic and positive.

Resolve conflicts with teammates or coaches as quickly as possible.
Don't let conflicts build up inside. Take action to resolve them. Express your complaint or resolve your conflict with the person who is responsible for the situation and can alter it. Don't gripe or complain to others, venting your feelings—that just spreads negative energy. If you respond to a conflict responsibly and immediately, it will have a little effect on your inner state and performance. But the longer it persists, the more you endanger your inner state and, hence, your performance.

Get your attitude and disposition right before going to practice or games.
Once you arrive for play, it's often too late to adjust your attitude. The real pro arrives with the right frame of mind, ready to play his or her best.

Don't be a loudmouth or show-off.
Neither one will produce many friends on a team. Quiet confidence, sincerity, and the ability to listen will serve you much better. The experience of team spirit is most generally described by players as the feelings of closeness between team members. Removing your facades and allowing others to know who and what you are is an important step in feeling close.

Go out of your way to help your teammates whenever you can.
Being mutually interdependent on each other stimulates team spirit. When you help someone, they feel closer and more responsive to you.

Be fully responsible for yourself.
Don't get into the habit of blaming others for your poor performances. Blaming the coach or your teammates when things don't go well serves no useful purpose. Work within positive

(Continued)

(Continued)

and constructive channels to produce needed changes. Blaming only serves to frustrate team harmony-building efforts.

Be your own best igniter.
Don't rely on others to push you from behind to keep you going. Self-starters are extremely valuable team members. They often become the triggers for positive momentum. Be a model of positive energy.

Communicate clearly, honestly, and openly with your coach.
To achieve a high level of team harmony, the communication between you and your coach must be healthy. The better you understand each other, the better your chances are of performing well.

Don't forget to have fun!
Being able to laugh and to loosen up a little often breaks down barriers and helps people to relax and feel closer. Remember, when you can enjoy, you can perform.

COPYRIGHT © 2008 DOMINO'S PIZZA ENTERPRISES, AUSTRALIA. REPRINTED BY PERMISSION. To customize this document, download this form to your hard drive from www.hiretheamericandream.com. The document can then be opened, edited, and printed using Microsoft Word or another popular word processing application.

■ SECTION 3. EMPLOYEE ATTITUDE AND BEHAVIOR

➤ Thirty-Day Expectations

There are many ways to make new employees feel comfortable when they join your team. In my franchise, one of those ways is to ensure that a peer-level employee conducts an interview with the applicant so that they have a realistic job preview and that, once they start working, there is someone in the store who becomes a de facto mentor to them. That creates a warm and welcoming environment.

Executive vice president of PeopleFirst at Domino's, Patti Wilmot, agrees. "It's important that you give a very clear picture of what the job entails," she says. "People in any job need to know what they're getting into. For a pizza store job, you can ask a candidate if they're willing to work Fridays until 2 A.M. and if they are willing to turn around and be back at the store by noon on Saturday. Sometimes, that's what it takes."

Any human resources professional will tell you that you are likely to lose a new employee in the first two weeks if he or she feels uncomfortable, doesn't know what's expected, or isn't provided with the training needed to succeed.

"Many companies lose hourly employees within their first 80 hours of work," Patti says, "usually because the employees don't have a clear expectation of the job or because the manager doesn't do a good job welcoming them. In the restaurant industry, we talk about turnover as if we have to accept it, and we don't. If you can give people a clear picture of the job and make them feel welcome, you've done more than most."

At my franchise, all team members receive a document we call "30-Day Expectations for New Team Members." It tells them succinctly what we expect their skill level to be after 30 days on the job. If they have trouble understanding something, either their peer mentor or their manager will be there to help them. This simple list of expectations has made the jobs less daunting and less mysterious. I'm reprinting our list here. You can use this idea to create a "30-Day List" for your employees.

EMPLOYEE 30-DAY LIST (DOWNLOADABLE)

Delivery Team Member Responsibilities

1. Be knowledgeable of boundaries and map of delivery area.
2. Be capable of professional interaction with the customer.
3. Be able to delight the customer, and demonstrate that you know how to resolve a customer concern.
4. Be in perfect uniform and ready to work at scheduled time.
5. Remember to dispatch and check in 100 percent of the time.
6. Perform safe deliveries 100 percent of the time.
7. No riding on the sidewalk. Always wear a helmet.
8. Use *heightened time awareness* (HTA). Call times out/in.
9. Make drops after each run; always have enough change.
10. Maintain your bicycle in safe and good working condition.
11. Have the Domino's picture ID and logo with number on bike.
12. Stay busy, help around store, and keep all areas clean and neat.

General Team Member Responsibilities

1. Know our menu, our pricing, our current offers, and our current TV advertising.
2. Be able to implement the two-minute drill.
3. Demonstrate how to set up the three-compartment sink.
4. Demonstrate how to properly wash, rinse, and sanitize dishes.
5. Attach box-top fliers and fold boxes.
6. Know the location of the MSDS forms.
7. Know the Domino's Pizza Product & Service Guarantee.

Cross-Training Skills

1. Demonstrate how to make breadsticks.
2. Demonstrate how to sauce and box buffalo wings.
3. Know all the topping codes.
4. Demonstrate how to top single- and double-portion pizzas.
5. Be able to properly post slips.
6. Know the arrangement of stock in the walk-in cooler, how to rotate stock, and how to identify what stock to use next.

Skills to Be Learned Later Include

1. Order taking
2. Topping multiple-topping pizzas
3. Slapping and saucing pizzas

➤ "I Promise"

One of the ways I've found to get team members to buy in to your policies and procedures is to explain those policies, train your employees until they demonstrate an understanding of them, then to get them to agree, in writing, to abide by them. At my stores, we don't consider this a contract, although some could interpret it that way. Instead, we ask our team members to *promise* to abide by the policies and procedures. For my employees, and I would think for yours, too, putting their signature on a document says something about their character. If they sign it, they believe in it. Here is a sample of an "I Promise" form used at my 89th Street shop.

"I PROMISE" FORM (DOWNLOADABLE)

I Promise

➤ To make sure the order is complete and properly dispatched every time.

➤ To call out the time in the oven, call out the time out the door, and call out the delivery time on every single pizza.

➤ To treat the customer with courtesy and respect in every situation.

➤ To help the store increase sales by promoting our products at every opportunity.

➤ To commit myself to increasing the knowledge of my job through training.

➤ To provide our customers with a *wow* experience every time!

➤ To observe all safety and security policies and conduct myself in such a way as to avoid accidents.

➤ To do my best to help make our store the best Domino's Pizza store in Manhattan.

Signed:

Printed name:

*COPYRIGHT © 2009 DAVE MELTON. To customize this document, download this form to your hard drive from www.hiretheamericandream.com. The document can then be opened, edited, and printed using Microsoft Word or another popular word processing application.

➤ The Integrity Letter

The largest Domino's Pizza franchise in the United States, RPM Pizza, provides all of its new employees with a 50-page booklet designed to answer all of their questions and provide information about the franchise's policies and procedures. RPM Pizza's booklet also shares the company's philosophies, values, and attitudes. RPM Pizza was founded by Richard P. Mueller Jr. in 1983 and today operates 140 stores in Mississippi and Louisiana. The franchise is led by Glenn Mueller, president and CEO, and Richard P. Mueller III, chief operating officer. Included in their new booklet is a letter to all employees about the concept of integrity, which should be a core value for any organization. Their letter can serve as a great model for you.

SAMPLE LETTER (DOWNLOADABLE)

We Demand Integrity
As part of the Domino's Pizza team, integrity matters—integrity protects you, your team, the company, and our customers. Your actions matter and have consequences. To operate a five-star, world-class, Great Company, we must operate in a friendly, safe, honest, drug-free, alcohol-free, nonabusive, and nondiscriminatory environment. Our policies, and, if broken, consequences, are outlined here.

Safe Harbor
RPM Pizza LLC is a people-first company. Should you have a financial problem, drug/alcohol problem, or have difficulty with abusive-type behavior, you may inform your supervisor or call the toll-free number and speak with Glenn or Richard Mueller III. This safe harbor has limitations, but is meant to help Team Members and to protect everyone. The company reserves the right to determine the best course of action to protect you and the company. A leave of absence, additional counseling at the Team Member's expense, or additional training may be set up as a requirement to continue working.

Your Rights to be Treated Fairly
➤ You will receive written policies on your pay, bonus, and benefits programs.
➤ You will be paid for all hours worked and all bonuses, per written policy.

(Continued)

(Continued)

➤ You will be treated with respect. When problems occur, you have the right and obligation to tell your manager/supervisor.
➤ You have the right to use the Team Member Feedback (TMF) System and are encouraged to do so if your manager/supervisor does not treat you fairly. You will not be retaliated against for complaining or using the TMF System.

Must-Dos by You and Each Team Member
➤ You must comply with our integrity and safety policies.
➤ You must let us know when a problem exists should the TMF System not work to your satisfaction.

Your Failure to Comply with Integrity and Safety Policies
After failing a drug test, receiving a DUI-type conviction, or an investigation in which you were found to use abusive behavior or violate integrity policies, you will be terminated from employment.

Team Member Feedback Is Protected
Ninety-nine percent of all problems can be resolved by talking to your General Manager and/or Regional Operations Director or Managing Director. The experienced team in your store and in your area has many interests to balance. We are not perfect, and when a problem occurs, let us know so we can fix it. If promises are not kept, use the TMF System. It works!

If you see any illegal activity or behavior that is against company policy, please let your General Manager or District Manager know immediately. If the behavior continues, use the TMF System, which is available 24 hours a day 7 days a week. If you or anyone's safety is in jeopardy or an illegal activity exists, immediately contact the police, your General Manager, District Manager and Domino's security hotline. A cash reward of up to $5,000 exists for any Team Member helping to give information for the arrest and conviction of anyone committing a crime on Domino's property or against any Domino's Team Member. Team Members providing feedback are protected, and some may receive a cash reward.

Our Commitment to You
We will work hard to make RPM Pizza, LLC a five-star, World Class, Great Company—which includes making it the best pizza company in the world to work with. We ensure each Team Member we hire has the opportunity for development and training to be the best Team Member. Your ideas, suggestions, comments, problems, and concerns are important. Please feel free to talk with us whenever we visit your store or to contact us by phone or e-mail. Thank you!

Glenn Mueller, President, CEO
Chief Excellence Officer
Richard Mueller III, COO
Richard P. Mueller, Founder

➤ RPM Pizza's Philosophies, Values, Attitudes

Included in RPM Pizza's Team Member booklet is a section on the franchise's philosophies, values, and attitudes, or PVAs. Not only are these important items covered in orientation programs, they are reinforced regularly throughout the year. Managers in the organization are even tested on their PVA knowledge. I admire the incredible detail they cover in this document, which is a direct reflection of the PVAs of the Mueller family itself.

RPM PIZZA FRANCHISE PHILOSOPHIES, VALUES, AND ATTITUDES (DOWNLOADABLE)

Putting People First. At RPM Pizza LLC, We Will . . .

➤ Make safety our number one priority.

➤ Strive to provide the best overall pay and benefits possible for our Team.

➤ Insist on a safe, drug-free work environment.

➤ Assist Team Members in need through the Partners Foundation and Team Member Assistance Program.

➤ Provide opportunity for our management team to franchise.

➤ Value diversity and strive to have a balanced team.

➤ Give our Team Members timely, constructive performance evaluations.

➤ Provide equal opportunity for employment and advancement.

➤ Seek out and share best practices with our team from inside and outside of our industry.

➤ Create an environment that inspires a passionate pursuit of excellence.

➤ Have the safest drivers on the road. We conduct semiannual Motor Vehicle Record checks.

➤ Use a quality management process to maximize our Team Members' level of success.

➤ Call each person who works for us "Team Member." All Team Members are equal; no Team Member is more important than another.

➤ Have owners and leadership team who keep an "open door" to all Team Members and are active in the business. They regularly tour stores to keep in contact with management Team Members.

➤ Strive to be a company that people are excited about so that they encourage family members and friends to apply for positions and participate in company events.

➤ Encourage our Team Members toward self-improvement, including physical fitness, personal learning, and social and spiritual development.

➤ Require strict grooming standards, hair restraint, jewelry, cleanliness, uniforms to conform to health regulations and standards.

Demanding Integrity. At RPM Pizza LLC, We Will . . .

➤ Practice the Golden Rule. Treat others the way we want to be treated.
➤ Not lie, cheat, steal; nor tolerate anyone who does.
➤ Put our promises and agreements in writing.
➤ Empower Team Members to make decisions with proper guidance utilizing our company PVAs.
➤ Never falsify paperwork, hide errors, overstate inventories, float tills, or steal from the store or company.

Striving to Make Every Customer a Loyal Customer. At RPM Pizza LLC, We Will . . .

➤ Always capitalize the "C" in Customer, emphasizing the importance of the people paying our paycheck!
➤ Empower our team. Every Team Member should be able to make a decision that will meet the Customer's expectation.
➤ Listen to our Customers. Using a feedback system, we must hear what the Customer is saying and react to it.
➤ Go beyond meeting the Customer's needs.
➤ *Wow* the Customer!
➤ Guarantee 100 percent Customer Satisfaction or we will gladly remake their order or refund their money.
➤ Continuously build market share with the goal to become number one in all markets.
➤ Accept all competitor coupons.
➤ Use only 100 percent real dairy cheese and natural ingredients, no artificial or cereal fillers in our meat products.
➤ Empower Team Members to honor our Product Guarantee—a full refund or replacement.

(Continued)

(Continued)

Delivering with Smart Hustle and Positive Energy. At RPM Pizza LLC, We Will . . .

➤ Earn a reputation of "the safest, most courteous drivers on the road" and wear seat belts both on and off the clock.
➤ Follow 100 percent of our security processes (including deposit procedures).
➤ Have *heightened time awareness* (HTA)—all positions.
➤ Answer phones on the first ring.
➤ Use the systematic program of Total Quality Management, striving for continuous improvement at all times.
➤ Promote teamwork and fun.
➤ Have the world's fastest pizza makers, who will make pizzas in one minute.
➤ Encourage all Team Members to hustle.
➤ Have the community and government consider us a great example of what a business should be.
➤ Build excitement at the store level with crew incentives.

Winning by Improving Results Every Day! At RPM Pizza LLC, We Will . . .

➤ Receive the freshest and most consistent products available from the Supply Chain Center twice a week.
➤ Require all Regional Operations Directors, District Managers, General Managers, and Senior Assistant Managers to complete the Serv-Safe class.
➤ Teach hands-on product training in every Assistant Manager class.
➤ Deliver using state-of-the-art heated bags to ensure our products are delivered at 170 degrees.
➤ Have the best equipment and tools to give the best product and service to our customers.
➤ Use the highest quality, freshest ingredients, which are better than those of our competitors.

➤ RPM Pizza's Request, Promise to Its Team Members

This last piece from RPM Pizza addresses specifically how the company would like its team members to treat customers, its colleagues, and the company itself.

WE PERSONALLY REQUEST THAT YOU . . . (DOWNLOADABLE)

➤ Always treat each Customer with respect.
➤ Provide each Customer their money's worth in a well-made product and prompt, courteous service.
➤ Resolve any problem that might arise to the Customer's satisfaction.
  ➤ You have the ability to determine if a Customer is happy with us or not.
  ➤ You have the ability to make sure the Customer decides to order from Domino's Pizza again.
  ➤ Treat our Customers, as you would like to be treated, with respect.

Always Treat Fellow Team Members with Respect

➤ Report to work as scheduled.
➤ Use "please" and "thank you."
➤ Give your best efforts to do your job the way it's supposed to be done.
➤ Make our stores a great place to work.
➤ Treat your fellow Team Members with respect.

Always Be Honest in Your Dealings with Us, Fellow Team Members, and the Company

➤ We do not, and will not, steal from you—so please never steal from us.
➤ Ring up all sales, collect payment for all transactions, and turn in all money received.
➤ Don't take free food or give free food to others.

(Continued)

(Continued)

➤ Be honest in reporting your times worked and give a full hour of work for each hour of pay.

➤ Stealing is an insidious disease that erodes personal dignity, integrity, and self-esteem. It also erodes a company's well-being. If $20 of food or money is stolen (or given away) from each RPM Pizza store each day, that amounts to over a million dollars lost per year companywide! Yes, each theft adds up to big losses. That loss reduces our company's ability to upgrade your store, replace worn equipment, and provide Team Member training classes.

➤ For RPM Pizza to be the World's Greatest Pizza Company, we must be a company in which stealing is nonexistent and honesty is practiced by all—in other words, a company in which everyone practices the Golden Rule.

We Personally Promise to Do Our Utmost to . . .

➤ Treat every Team Member we encounter with respect and honesty, and encourage all other Team Members to do the same.

➤ Make RPM Pizza LLC the World's Greatest Pizza Company—which includes making it the best pizza company in the world to work for.

➤ Make ourselves available to hear your ideas, suggestions, comments, problems, or concerns.

➤ Valley Pizza, Inc.: "Your Image = *Our Image*"

Valley Pizza, Inc., is a terrific franchise operated by my friend Tony Osani, who is one of the few Domino's Pizza franchisees who have been inducted into the Chairman's Circle Hall of Fame. Like RPM Pizza, Tony provided me with his entire new team member orientation manual. One of the items I'm including here is Valley Pizza's explanation of how one individual's image reflects on the entire organization.

YOUR IMAGE = *OUR* IMAGE (DOWNLOADABLE)

How Do I Fit In?
As a Domino's Pizza team member, you need a positive, winning attitude. These tips will help you be a winner:

- ➤ Greet each customer in a cheerful, upbeat manner.
- ➤ Speed is inside the store! Customers are impressed with efficiency, enthusiasm, and hustle.
- ➤ Maintain a friendly, courteous attitude.
- ➤ Be personable and don't forget to smile!
- ➤ Handle customer concerns in a friendly manner.
- ➤ Drive safely and professionally. Your safety and your customers depend on it.
- ➤ Join with other team members to keep a clean store.

➤ "Presentation and Attitude Are Everything"

This is another great piece of work I got from the files of my mentor, Frank Meeks, who loved the art of public relations.

HOW YOU PRESENT YOURSELF AND YOUR PRODUCT ARE THE BIGGEST PART OF PR! HERE ARE A FEW THINGS TO KEEP IN MIND (DOWNLOADABLE)

➤ People will decide if they like you within two minutes of meeting you.

➤ Make eye contact and smile!

➤ Yes, people will judge you by your handshake. Give people a firm handshake and look them in the eye.

➤ If people like you, they'll look for reasons to say yes to you.

➤ If they don't like you, they'll look for reasons to say no.

➤ People respond to positive appearances—clean clothes and good posture go a long way!

➤ Attitude is:
  ➤ Body language—55%
  ➤ Voice tone—38%
  ➤ Word use—7%

➤ Negative words create a negative message. Avoid words like *don't* and *not*.
  ➤ Instead of saying, "Don't hesitate to call," say, "Please give us a call."
  ➤ Instead of saying "Not a problem," simply say, "You're welcome."

➤ Avoid closed body language.
  ➤ No crossing arms.
  ➤ No looking down.

➤ Color coordination is 30 percent more likely to get you a sale!
  ➤ Color coordination with your product or the person with whom you're selling is easy on the consumer's eye.
  ➤ Primary colors or cool colors (blue, green, purple) are also easy on the consumer's eye.

FROM THE ARCHIVES OF DOMINO'S PIZZA TEAM WASHINGTON. To customize this document, download this form to your hard drive from www.hiretheamericandream.com. The document can then be opened, edited, and printed using Microsoft Word or another popular word processing application.

➤ Valley Pizza's "Personal Conduct Expectations"

As you've likely noticed by now, a number of common themes have appeared in this section and throughout the book. In order to help make entry-level team members successful, you have to start by providing them with clear expectations, tips for how they can meet those expectations, and information about how questions, issues, and concerns will be addressed. Tony Osani provides all of his new employees with a list of expectations he has of his team members.

PERSONAL CONDUCT EXPECTATIONS
(DOWNLOADABLE)

At Domino's Pizza we strive to provide each team member with a pleasant working atmosphere consistent with the rights and welfare of other workers and with the company's obligation to effectively manage the business. To this end, we have established these minimum standards of personal conduct in the hope that no one will endanger the well-being, health, safety, or property of a fellow team member or the company.

The Following Are Expectations We Have of You:

- ➤ Drive in a safe manner at all times.
- ➤ Comply with company safety, fire prevention, health, and security rules.
- ➤ On company property or on company time, never use alcohol or illegal drugs; do not use prescription or over-the-counter drugs that may cause drowsiness or slow your reaction time.
- ➤ Never possess firearms or other weapons on company property or on company time.

(Continued)

(Continued)

➤ Never strike or threaten to strike any person on company property or on company time.
➤ Never make false, fraudulent, or malicious statements about the company, team members, customers, or suppliers.
➤ Handle company funds or property in a safe, responsible manner.
➤ Come to work on time, in uniform, ready to work.
➤ Never engage in gambling or disorderly or immoral conduct while on company property or business.
➤ Act responsibly toward other team members, customers, suppliers, and so forth.

■ SECTION 4. EXCEPTIONAL CUSTOMER SERVICE

Serving customers is not a punishment; it is a privilege. That's how I want my team members to think. Customers form the foundation of how my employees make money to support their families. The more delighted customers we have, the more opportunities my team members have to take care of the people most important to them. That's why we never stop talking about customer service. This final section is dedicated to some of the tools we use to continually remind our team about how important the customer is to all of us.

CUSTOMER SERVICE: THE FACTS (DOWNLOADABLE)

➤ It costs six times more to attract a new customer than it does to keep an existing one.
➤ Typically, a disappointed customer will tell 8 to 10 people about their problem.
➤ Seven out of ten complaining customers will do business with you again if you resolve the complaint in their favor.
➤ Of those customers who quit, 68 percent will do so because of an attitude of indifference by the company or by a specific individual.
➤ In summary, all of these facts say: Customer Satisfaction = Success!

COPYRIGHT © 2009 DAVE MELTON. To customize this document, download this form to your hard drive from www.hiretheamericandream.com. The document can then be opened, edited, and printed using Microsoft Word or another popular word processing application.

■ TOTAL CUSTOMER SERVICE PROGRAM

We routinely call our stores posing as real customers and order pizza to see how our customer service reps are doing. Sometimes, when we're in the stores, we'll listen to how they handle orders from real customers. We audit them using a form we call the Total Customer Service Program and use this as a training tool.

TOTAL CUSTOMER SERVICE PROGRAM REVIEW FORM (DOWNLOADABLE)

Introduction

➤ Did you thank the customer for choosing us?
➤ Did you introduce yourself?

(Continued)

(Continued)

➤ Did you speak clearly?
➤ Did you have a "smile" in your voice?
➤ If the customer was put on hold, did you include a free topping?

Selling Pizza

➤ Were you knowledgeable about our offers?
➤ Did you suggestive-sell?
➤ Did you make sure the customer had something to drink with his or her meal?
➤ Did you tell the customer about any new products?

Leaving the Customer with a Smile

➤ Did you price perfectly?
➤ Did you inform the customer that the price includes tax?
➤ Did you inform the customer of the time he or she ordered and the service guarantee?
➤ Did you thank the customer for his or her order and offer future assistance?

■ COMMITMENT TO THOROUGH PREPARATION

Every phone call might be the first order of a major rush, so it is important that we are prepared well in advance. We don't want to be running around trying to get the store prepped for business when business is already happening. We have all of our managers follow through this checklist before opening for business each day.

PREPARATION (DOWNLOADABLE)

Phone area, customer area, counter, and front windows should be kept clean and sparkling at all times.

The following items should be available near the phone counter:

➤ Street list showing street numbers served within the delivery boundaries.
➤ A list of emergency numbers, including:
  ➤ 911 and the local police precinct non-emergency number
  ➤ The manager's home phone number
  ➤ Dave Melton's home and cell phone numbers
  ➤ Domino's Safety Hotline
  ➤ Phone numbers and delivery areas of other nearby Domino's Pizza stores for customers who live outside of this store's delivery area
  ➤ A calculator
  ➤ A pen secured to the counter and paper to write on
  ➤ Information concerning the current local and national promotions
➤ The napkin holder and straw holder should be filled at all times.
➤ The menu holders inside and outside should always be filled with menus or flyers. The holders should be clean and replaced if damaged.
➤ Any trash on the sidewalk and 18 inches into the street off the curb should be picked up. All team members should be conscious of the physical image that our store projects to customers who walk past our store.
➤ All equipment should be clean, operable, and neatly arranged.
➤ Make sure all telephones are clean and in good working order.
➤ A supply of white glue should be available for box-topping pizza boxes.
➤ Enough pizza boxes for the day should be folded, topped, and stored.
➤ Glass cleaner and cleaning rags should be available for continuous cleaning when you're not answering phones.

RULES OF ROUTING (DOWNLOADABLE)

These Rules of Routing are established to provide the customer with the best service possible and to dispatch deliveries in a manner fair and equitable to each delivery person.

- ➤ The oldest run is to be dispatched first.
- ➤ An order is not a run until the entire order is complete; for example, both pies of a two-pie are run are ready to leave the store.
- ➤ Close runs should be dispatched singly and delivered on foot. All delivery people on foot are expected to hustle (jog) while on delivery.
- ➤ Runs will be doubled up when two runs are distant from the store, close to each other, and sufficient time exists to enable both pies to be delivered quickly. Assignment of a double run will take several facts into consideration:
  - ➤ Will the best interests of each customer be served?
  - ➤ What is the reputation of hustle of this delivery person?
  - ➤ What is the experience of this delivery person?
  - ➤ How many runs are presently in the store?
  - ➤ How many delivery people are on the road?
  - ➤ How soon are delivery people expected to return?
  - ➤ What are the distance, proximity, and times of the orders?
  - ➤ Can we get in and out of these buildings quickly?
- ➤ Input from delivery people regarding multiple runs may be considered, but for any multiple run, management approval is required.
- ➤ Management's decision on routing is final.
- ➤ Runs are to be routed and dispatched when they are ready, without regard to who is up next. No favoritism or discrimination is to occur. Teamwork is expected to be displayed. Fair and equitable assignment of runs will occur over the long term. Some days, a person may get a lot of long runs and other days will get many short ones.
- ➤ Any complaining or arguments concerning the assignments of runs will be looked on unfavorably by management and can affect rate of pay, promotions, and schedules.

(Continued)

HOW TO TURN *OW* INTO *WOW!*

A few years ago, I had a meeting of all of my managers, customer service representatives, pizza makers, and delivery drivers. The objective: I wanted them to talk openly about the top reasons customers call our stores back with a problem, and more important, what they—the team members—thought they should do to handle these customers. I believed that by having my team identify the problems, and the solutions, they would be more likely to follow through on them. And it worked.

We called the finished document, "How to Turn a Customer's *Ow* into a *Wow*." Very candidly, here are the top four reasons people call us to complain and how we believe we should address those complaints.

**COMMON CUSTOMER COMPLAINTS AND SOLUTIONS
(DOWNLOADABLE)**

"I ordered a pizza about 30 (or more) minutes ago, and it hasn't arrived yet."
You should:

1. Apologize for the delay.

(Continued)

(Continued)

2. Find out how old the pizza is and when it left the store.
3. Determine who the delivery person is.
4. Give an estimate to the customer about when he or she can expect the pizza.
5. Inform the customer of our Product & Service Guarantee.
6. Call the customer back in 10 minutes to be sure the order has arrived.
7. Apologize again, and leave your name with the customers, asking them to call and ask for you if they need to call back.

"I just received my pizza, and the driver forgot my Cokes (or side item, second pizza, etc.)"
You should:

1. Apologize for the inconvenience.
2. Determine exactly what is missing, and send the replacement item immediately.
3. Have the delivery person bring something extra for free, like a couple of soft drinks or bread sticks.
4. Retrain delivery person to read tickets more carefully (management may decide to highlight extra items on the order ticket for additional visibility).
5. Assure the customer that we will perform as promised in the future.
6. Call the customer back in 10 minutes to be sure the order has arrived.
7. Apologize again, and leave your name with the customer; ask the customer to call and ask for you if he or she needs to call back.

"The delivery person (manager, phone person) was rude."
You should:

1. Apologize.
2. Connect the customer with a manager.

3. Determine what happened from the customer's perspective.
4. Address and resolve the customer's problem.
5. Assure the customer that the manager will talk to the rude employee.
6. Assure the customer that our company will not tolerate rudeness from our team members.
7. Apologize again, and leave your name with the customers, asking them to call and ask for you if they need to call back.
8. Talk to the team member, and retrain or discipline as appropriate (including termination).

"I got the wrong order."
You should:

1. Apologize.
2. Find out what needs to be done to make it right.
3. Redeliver the correct order *immediately.*
4. Tell the customers they can keep the incorrect order if they desire, plus the correct order.
5. Give the customers something for free, like soft drinks or bread sticks.
6. If appropriate, give the customers the entire order for free.
7. Call them back after the correct delivery is made to be sure their order is correct.
8. Apologize again, and leave your name with the customers, asking them to call and ask for you if they need to call back.

FINAL THOUGHTS

Being able to fulfill my dream of being an entrepreneur, owning my own business, becoming a millionaire, and helping others to do the same makes me feel more blessed than I can truly express. More than that, having the opportunity to work with so many willing and dedicated team members who joined my team after coming to this country or who entered the workforce for their first job, watching them grow personally and professionally to enter the American middle class, and beyond, means more to me than you can ever imagine. Dreams really do come true

I hope you have found something in this book worthwhile—something that you can take and introduce into your own business that will help you turn your entry-level, minimum-wage workforce into a loyal, dedicated, high-performance, customer-delighting team.

I'd love to hear your ideas and what you think of this book. Please write to me at davidm790@aol.com. Thank you for reading my book, and here's wishing you success in *Hiring the American Dream!*

—Dave Melton

Index